Get Out Of Your Own Way!

Danielle—
You Rock!
Let me know what you
think & keep Rocking
it — Bob

HOW TO BREAK THE PERFECTIONIST MINDSET AND UNLEASH THE FLOODGATES OF PROSPERITY FOR YOUR BUSINESS.

WWW.OUTOFYOURWAYBOOK.COM

Written By
Bob McIntosh

Edited By
Amanda Pawelski

A FREE GIFT TO SAY THANK YOU

I am truly honored that you would choose to pick up this book and read it. I know that your time is extremely valuable and the fact that you found my experiences worthy of spending that time means the world to me. I would like to repay that favor in a small way with this little bonus for those who buy the book!

I interviewed a number of very successful business owners, people doing 6, 7, 8 and even 9 figures a year in their businesses about the idea of getting out of their own way and what it meant for them. I know that they have mastered this concept as you don't grow businesses of that size without first figuring out how to get out of your own way.

These folks time is often worth over $1,000/hour but you have the opportunity to be there with me as I ask them questions about their own businesses and how they achieved their success.

To get exclusive access to these bonus interviews, head over to *www.outofyourwaybook.com/interviews*

Where to Find Stuff

Acknowledgements

There are several people without whom this book would never have been written. First and foremost I want to thank my parents. No matter what, they were always the ones telling me that I could do or be anything I wanted. They supported me through all the ups and downs I have faced and I appreciate them more than words could ever describe. When you tell a child they can do or be anything and support that with your actions you will be surprised what they can achieve. Secondly I want to thank Fortune Builders and Mind Protein for without their coaching and mentorship I would never have written this book. Never underestimate the importance of both amazing coaches and amazing mentors. They can propel you to levels you never dreamed of before. Amanda, thank you for editing this and taking my poor grammar and polishing it to a shine! Lastly, I want to thank YOU, the reader of this book. While it's pretty awesome to say I am an author, if no one actually reads this book, takes the actions I recommend and improves their lives and businesses then what was the point. So thank you for considering your time worthy of my experiences.

CHAPTER ONE

Why Are You Here?

Here you are, about to start down a path of growth and take a precipitous exit out of your comfort zone. Do you remember what brought you to this point? What drove you to take this giant step forward?

I remember having a little bit of money left over after college and needing to decide how to best use it. After some weighing of options, and after reading numerous books, I decided that I wanted to start down the path of real estate investment. Of course, if you had told me at that point in time where I would ultimately end up— writing this book, standing on stage and speaking to large crowds, meeting the best mentors and coaches one could ask for, and more— I would have promptly taken you to a shrink, because the only conclusion would have been lunacy. However, there was a breakthrough moment, while reading Rich Dad, Poor Dad, when it all just clicked.

I come from an entrepreneurial family, so I always kind of thought that it would be natural to start my own business; however, it was in that moment that it clicked, and I told myself, "I am going to do it!" It would take a few more years of working my full time job before I finally broke free and began pursuing a public speaking career, continuing with real estate investment, but I will never forget that first big "a-ha" moment.

Do you remember your own big moment? Do you remember when you decided you were going to take that plunge? How did you feel? Were you excited? Were you terrified? Were you exuberant and light headed? I felt all of these emotions and then some, but the emotion that trumped the rest was a feeling of destiny! I felt as if, no matter what happened next, it was supposed to be. It hasn't been easy, and there have been casualties along the way. It took longer than I would have ever anticipated, and it was more difficult than I ever would have thought possible, but I can stand here now knowing that despite everything, I wouldn't change a thing. Not one single thing.

Wherever you are on your own journey, take a moment to reflect on that moment when you made the decision to free yourself from the corporate chains and pursue building your own business. Relish in how that moment made you feel. As entrepreneurs, we are often so focused on the future that we forget to reflect every once in a while. Once you have given that moment due consideration, we can begin!

Now, like many people, I started my working career with a full-time job. Though that job wasn't inherently bad, it would also never set me free. It never allowed me the freedoms that I craved: the freedom to choose my own schedule, the freedom of time, the freedom to pursue projects I am passionate about, the freedom to choose my own path and create my own destiny, and, indeed, the freedom that now allows me to write this very book. Freedom cannot be obtained while working for someone else; my craving for freedom is what ultimately led me down the path of entrepreneurship.

But it wasn't easy. I began my entrepreneurship like many others before me, working a day job to pay the bills—too terrified to leave for loss of money—spending nights and weekends creating my own business. Many have followed this same path, and for most people, starting in this manner makes sense, especially if you have others that are dependent upon you. It is nearly impossible to just give up the lifestyle to which you have become accustomed in order to pursue a dream. Instead of jumping into the unknown, we take sensible steps, working little by little, step by step.

My full-time job required that I work an average of 50 to 60 hours a week not counting the additional 10 hours consumed by travel. This schedule left me with very few hours to dedicate to my own business. I was constantly having to fight the "too much to do, not enough time" uphill battle that is all too common of our driven peers. Lack of time led me to the idea at the core of my own business practice, and which I now share with you: Done is Better than Perfect.

When you don't have time, you can't worry about perfection. Simply put, there isn't enough time for it. Ironically, whenever I leave perfection behind—in my business, my job, or my personal life—I see better results, bigger forward leaps, and greater breakthroughs. I achieve more success.

It is my sincere, honest hope that you too find success in your business life, personal life, and everything else you do. In fact I personally coach other entrepreneurs to greater levels of success and am proud to know that I helped them get there! Great entrepreneurs are always learning, and I believe that the knowledge contained in this book is life changing. Done is Better than Perfect has changed my life, and I know that it can change your life by closing that seemingly insurmountable gap between your current state and your end goal of becoming a successful entrepreneur.

By sharing these leaps and experiences with you, I will show you how you can achieve the Done is Better than Perfect mindset, and apply it to your own business, no matter where you are in your journey.

Join me. Begin your new life. Learn to Get Out of Your Own Way and be the entrepreneur you were always meant to be!

Bob McIntosh

CHAPTER TWO

The Done Is Better Than Perfect Philosophy

What is 'Done is Better than Perfect'? Why should I care enough to read this book?

Let me tell you now: Done is Better than Perfect. It may seem like a perfectly simple concept, but the origins of this phrase, as well as its effects within your business, are truly profound.

During my time interacting with thousands of entrepreneurs, I have seen far too many who are struggling or failing. There are too many who are "succeeding," but not at the level to which they strive. There are too many who are on the verge of success, walking the line between achieving their goals and giving up, at the mercy of the next stiff breeze to push them one way or the other. There are too many who are only creating jobs for themselves when they could be creating jobs for others. There are too many who are scared to even start, not even in the game because they are too terrified to take the first steps in business development. There are also far too many who are just waiting for the "perfect time." This last group of people is the furthest from the idea of Done is Better than Perfect.

If you are always waiting for the perfect time, you will never reach your final destination. In terms of Done is Better than Perfect, and in terms of starting your own business as an entrepreneur, we need look no further than Kevin Spacey's character in the movie *Casino Jack*. Profoundly, insightfully, he says:

"People look at politicians and celebrities on TV, newspapers, glossy magazines. What do they see? 'I'm just like them.' That's what they see. 'I'm special.' 'I'm different.' 'I could be any one of them.' Well, guess what? You can't. You know why? Because, in reality, mediocrity is where most people live. Mediocrity is the elephant in the room. It's ubiquitous. Mediocrity is in your schools. It's in your dreams. It's in your family. Those of us who know this, those of us who understand this disease of the dull, we do something about it. We do more because we have to. The deck was always stacked against us. You are either a big leader or a slave chewing your way onto the C-train. I will not allow the world I touch to be vanilla."Another idea about the table d'hôte. A few weeks ago I was very cross with my dear wife at the dinner-table at a Tyrolese health resort, because she was not sufficiently reserved with some neighbors with whom I wished to have absolutely nothing to do. I begged her to occupy herself rather with me than with the strangers. That is just as if I had been at a disadvantage at the table d'hôte. The contrast between the behavior of my wife at the table and that of Mrs. E.L. in the dream now strikes me: "Addresses herself entirely to me."

I love this quote because it flawlessly describes our obsession with perfection. It may seem odd to call perfection "mediocrity," but when you are constantly striving for perfection you cannot obtain, you are, by default, stuck in mediocrity. Mediocrity is the ball to which your ankle is chained. The chain has just enough slack to give you the illusion of freedom and of progress, but if you go too far, the mediocrity ball will keep you in your place. It will keep you in check and ensure that you don't progress any further.

Perfectionism is the chain. It lets you think you are moving away from mediocrity, but it is only an illusion. The problem is you never know how much chain is left. You just keep walking and thinking that, if you can just get a little further, the ball of mediocrity won't be there. But that ball is always there, and your obsession with perfection is keeping you chained to it. The further you try to walk away from it, the more it has you pinned to the ground.

This is the problem with striving for perfection: you will never be perfect. No matter what you do, if you are constantly trying to achieve perfection, you will always be stuck in mediocrity. You will be stuck in one place, never achieving more, and never achieving what you could and should be doing. You will be stuck doing what you think your business needs, instead of making your business do what it needs to do for you. You MUST—not should, not think about, not maybe—you MUST break that chain. Before taking one more step, stop pulling against the dead weight of mediocrity, limiting yourself by the idea of perfection, and ditch the construct all together. Adopt the new construct and idea, Done is Better than Perfect, and begin your true path towards success.

I want to define this new idea for you more though, because it's important for you to have a clear understanding of Done is Better than Perfect before you read the rest of this book. It can be simplified to the idea that not everything needs to be 100% perfect. In fact, making sure that everything is perfect is a recipe for failure, especially when starting a business or trying to grow a business. Done is Better than Perfect will help you achieve more success than you already have.

Now, when I talk about Done is Better than Perfect, I want you to visualize a line. Imagine you are on a beach and draw a line in the sand. Go ahead. That line is the DBP line. That is the point at which you should be done working on whatever "it" is, and it doesn't matter what "it" is. Know when you are at that point. Once you cross that line, you are striving for perfection, and perfection becomes exponentially harder to achieve the closer you get to it.

The problem is that every time you take one step forward, that step gets smaller and smaller and smaller, so even though you may continue making progress towards perfection, you will never actually reach it. Each step taken will be smaller than the last one, and your goal will always be just out of reach. As a football team approaches the last 10 yards before a touchdown, it becomes harder and harder to get those last few yards. It takes more plays to gain fewer yards. Instead, rather than inching forward one yard at a time, throw the ball. Take control of the situation, and make that touch-down! You don't always get a second chance when you pass up an opportunity.

When I talk about Done is Better than Perfect and the idea of perfection, the 80/20 rule applies. Generally, 80% of your time will be spent working on that last 20% of your work while striving to achieve your idea of perfection. What does this mean in terms of business? Well, the 80/20 rule applies to many things. For example, you are going to find that getting things done to the point of the DBP line—the point at which you can call something done—will usually only take about 20% of your effort, possibly even less. The remaining 80% of your effort is what it would take to get to 100% perfect, which you will learn will never happen and will consume too much of your valuable time. You don't want to allow perfection to do that. It's not worth it.

Now, not every single thing you do will require exactly this ratio of effort—actually, for many entrepreneurs, the ratio will be closer to 90/10—but if you look at everything in the big picture, you will find this ratio will be true on average.

Naturally, I often get push back when someone first hears this idea, so I want to make one thing clear: **This is not an excuse to produce inferior work!** Your efforts should still be of high quality. Steve Jobs once said that no matter what you do, you should be "a yardstick of quality. Some people aren't used to an environment where excellence is expected."

Imagine if everything you do is a "yardstick of quality" against which others wish to measure themselves. This does not mean that you should do something just for the sake of doing it, but rather, when you do something, do it well. Just don't let perfection, or the idea of perfection, hold you back from completing it. Don't let that chain and ball stop you from moving forward just because "it" isn't perfect yet. Remember, it will probably never be perfect.

This reminds me of an anecdote: there was a person who felt she had been working to the utmost of her ability at her job. When the time came for her review, she was given a score of 3 out of 4 for every item, despite glowing reviews of everything she had done and accomplished in the past year. When she inquired as to why she hadn't received higher scores, she was told that *no one ever gets a 4 because no one is ever perfect. If you think you're perfect, you stop trying.*

No matter how big or small "it" may be, you need to define what success looks like, what the end result will be, for whatever it is you are working on. When you define what it means to get something done, whether it be starting your business, a project within your business, or even a goal within your project, you will have success.

For every person reading this book, success will be different. Success will be defined by you, not by anybody else. Success cannot be defined by your peers, your family, your friends, or your co-workers. Only you can define success for yourself.

I want you to think about what success means for you. For a lot of us, success means money, but money is usually only a means to something bigger and better; for example, money usually leads to the idea of freedom from or of something such as freedom of time, freedom of energy, and freedom of choice. What is it that you want from success? What is it that building your business will allow you to have that you don't currently have?

Remember, everyone will define success differently, so if you don't know what that definition is for you yet, I suggest that you stop reading for a few minutes, think about it, and try to define your success.

In fact, write it down right here:

_____

_____

_____

If you don't know what your success is yet, then you can't continue with this book in an effective manner.

Your definition of success will be your measuring guide. It should be the goal towards which you are working, and it doesn't have to be the end goal. In fact, you might find that once you reach your current success goal, you may rethink your success from that new vantage point and redefine your success to a goal that is further down the road. For many entrepreneurs, this is the case.

One of my favorite pieces of advice comes from Brendon Burchard—author, public speaker, and online trainer on the topics of motivation, high performance, and online marketing—and it goes something like this: Pick up your spear of purpose, throw that spear, and then start walking to where it is. That is your goal. Once you have reached it, pick it up again, and throw it again. Then, start walking towards it again. Reaching and picking up that spear, or achieving your goal, doesn't mean that everything is perfect, however; it just means you have achieved enough of your success to feel ready to "throw" it again and begin moving toward the next goal.

By continuingly picking up this spear, throwing it, and walking—or running—toward it, you are always moving forward. This is the most important element of starting a business. Always keep moving forward, no matter what, even if it's just at a crawl. Just like the 3rd place finisher in the 2015 Austin marathon, who collapsed just before the finish line and still crawled her away across that finish line, you must always keep moving forward.

Success, for many of you, will be defined in this same way. You've thrown your spear. It has landed at a point; it has drawn your line in the sand. You know where that point is now. Once you reach it, your true measure of success will be picking it up and throwing it further down the beach. Then, continue to do that over and over and over again.

Like most entrepreneurs, you will never be completely satisfied with where you have arrived once you get to that point. You will always want more, and that is okay. Never be afraid of wanting more and having more success. That is what defines you as an entrepreneur, and it is what makes you such a powerful person by allowing you to take the risks you need to take while starting and building companies.

Done is Better than Perfect doesn't always make sense. Truth be told, there are many times where this concept is flat-out wrong; for example, if you are a doctor, a pilot, or any other profession responsible for people's lives, you should not apply Done is Better than Perfect. To do so would be to put those lives at risk. This should be obvious, but I feel it's important to point out.

For entrepreneurs and business owners, however, this concept will help you be more successful. Unfortunately, you've been trained since a young age to achieve perfection, even though this is a detriment as an entrepreneur. As employees, this is usually fine and sometimes even encouraged, but as an entrepreneur, you need to take a step back and realize that done truly is better than perfect.

For now, I challenge you to think about your definition of success. I challenge you to think about how you will spend your time from now on. I challenge you to apply Done is Better than Perfect in your business practices. If you don't take on this challenge, you may never reach your full potential.

CHAPTER THREE

Why Do We Want Perfection So Bad?

Before diving into understanding your current mindset and changing that mindset in order to become more in line with necessary growth patterns, you first must analyze your obsession with perfection.

Where did it start? Why is it so hard for so many entrepreneurs to achieve what they want to achieve? Why is it difficult for many start-up businesses to get off the ground? Every single year, there are tens of thousands of businesses started, and every single year, nearly as many fail. In fact, almost 80% of all small business start-ups fail within the first five years. Why does this happen to so many new businesses?

People usually start out with great ideas and great intentions. Generally speaking, they tend to fall short when it comes to actually getting things done. Now, this does not apply to every single business; however, from what I have seen, this is the single most common factor for the 80% of businesses that fail.

In order to really understand where your obsession with perfection comes from, you must rewind the clock all the way back to infancy. From the very beginning, you are taught right from wrong and good from bad, and you are praised every time you do something better than the last time. Once you reach kindergarten, you begin to receive grades based on how well you perform different tasks. It is in this arena that testing reinforces the idea of perfectionism. As you are awarded grades, based on a standard grade letter scale or on a percentage scale, you become conditioned to push and strive for the A or the 100%. In fact, anything less is generally considered bad or inferior.

Your perfectionism conditioning is then further reinforced when you have to bring your grade reports home to your parents. Many schools require parents to sign these report cards as proof, not only that you showed your parents, but that they gave their final judgment of your school performance. Most children want to please their parents, and some children are given rewards at home for good grades, so their obsession with perfection becomes almost inevitable and unavoidable.

Your level of perfection was based on your report card. Depending on your upbringing and other variable factors, you may have been praised for your effort, but if straight A's were not listed, you were probably also encouraged to "try harder next time." You were praised for what the paper said rather than the amount of effort you put forth while achieving those grades. You were held in judgment of your performance comparative to the "perfect" A or 100% standard. You were always in competition with the best and the worst among your peers, ranked by your distance to that coveted spot of perfection.

This ranking system does not work for entrepreneurs. For most employees, the mentality of trying to be perfect still applies because they are trying to succeed within an already defined and established set of parameters. This book, however, is not for employees looking to be better at their nine-to-fives; this book is for those who want something more, those who want to create their own businesses, and those who want to enjoy the freedoms that come with achieving entrepreneurial successes. Yet, you have been taught from a very young age that this is not what you want. You have been taught to want perfection even though, in the real world, perfectionism is both largely unattainable and even, as you are now learning, a hindrance to successful entrepreneurial endeavors.

Considering how deeply engrained perfectionism is in our society, it is difficult at times to fathom how some people are able to break free and determine their own paths. In high school, for example, exemplars of perfectionism are dubbed the coveted titles Valedictorian and Salutatorian. These noted students have the highest grades and are largely considered to be the closest to perfect within their graduating class, even though they are not always the students who have truly learned the most. In fact, more often than not, I would argue that these students did not learn the most, at least not in a true and applicable sense. Instead, they demonstrated a mastery of memorization and fact regurgitation, and they subsequently thrived in our current education system. Determining how much information you can recite on command is not a great way to measure whether or not someone is truly learning and growing, and it is a horrible lesson for future entrepreneurs to learn.

As high school students, you are told that your future successes depend on which colleges you attend, which is dependent upon how close your grades are to perfect. You are told that there is no other path to success, no option other than striving for perfection. Your grades are one of the only concrete measurements by which you can claim your near perfection and stand apart from your less-perfect peers. Your grades determine where you fit in and the colleges to which you are eligible to apply. The message is made very clear: if you receive low grades, you won't stand a chance of success in life.

Perfectionism conditioning gets even worse after high school, continuing all the way through college. Future employers post rigid job requirements for all applicants to meet, and they want prospective employees to be as close to perfect as possible. GPA restrictions are an easy way to establish ranks. Grades have morphed into GPAs. The name and scale has changed, but the hierarchical construct remains the same. It sounds fancier, but, at the end of the day, it is the same thing. It is a measurement of perfection. The problem with grades, GPAs, and any other form of measurement in this batch system, is that they do not measure what you have actually learned, what mistakes you have made, and what level and type of growth you have experienced. True learning is much harder to judge objectively, so it is swept aside in favor of standardized tests and scores.

I like to call the process of memorizing information and spitting it back out Conveyor Brain Training (CBT.) Students are fed through the education machine on a conveyor belt, batched by age, which is realistically one of the worst ways to determine intelligence. We all know that people have differing intelligences when they are older, so why wouldn't this be true when they are younger as well? In fact, in addition to teaching and learning methodologies, most other traditional depictions and experiences of school are based on batch, or conveyer, methodology. Lunch is literally served on a conveyor belt in some cafeterias, or it is at least apportioned along an assembly line, because the batch method dictates that we all have the same dietary needs. Perhaps this "truth" is one of the factors resulting in rising childhood obesity rates.

Students progress through their days in school on a schedule, which is not unlike a conveyor belt. Class periods are always the same length of time, even though students may need additional assistance and time to focus on some subjects more than other subjects. Assignments are given to the entire class regardless of how equipped, prepared, or knowledgeable individual students may be within that class.

I can clearly recall an example of this from my own high school experience. It took place in an English course for which I had been registered. The teacher was comically old and wore glasses with thin frames secured by a chain that went around the back of her neck. Her lips were always pursed in a disappointed look. In retrospect, I believe the apparent disappointment was more likely the result of her own lacking accomplishments rather than general disappointment in her students; however, at the time, I always felt that she was disappointed with me.

As was, and still is, the case in many English classes in the United States, we often read aloud. In my particular class, there were several students who were, simply put, horrible at reading. I cannot speak to how intelligent they were, but I do know that they were horrible at reading, at least when that reading took place in front of our class. It may have just been that their nerves or their fear of public speaking would take over, but every time one of these students read, there was always a collective sigh from the rest of the students present. We knew, and most unfortunately, they knew, that the next several minutes would be filled with the painful dragging out of stuttered, mispronounced, and confused vocabulary.

I would say that my own reading ability was about average for my grade level. By that I mean that there were certainly students who were better than me, and there were certainly students who were not better than me. The problem with this batch method of class assignments and grade levels is that there is often a stark and dramatic difference between the above average and the below average students. Consider where you fit in within some of your classes. How obvious were the differences in student ability? Do you think the class was a good placement for all of the students in attendance? Was it a good placement for you?

Most people can recall experiences similar to my own high school example, and the situation does not change much after graduation. I recognize that this is not always the case, but many jobs, especially in big companies, are batched as well. If you are in an entry level position, rarely are you given an opportunity to show what you can truly bring to the table. You are perceived as having very little experience, regardless of whether or not that is true. You work in your cube, and you do your job until you move far enough along the conveyor belt to get bumped up to the next belt or position. For many people, this system continues for the next forty years of their lives. The owner of the conveyor belt may change, you may hop conveyors belts from time to time, but the machine remains the same. The realization of this fact encourages some people to make a change by breaking out of their current system and becoming entrepreneurs. In fact, that may be exactly what pushed you into action!

Perfection is a goal at the end of the conveyor belt. You are continuously moving along that conveyor belt, whether you are in school or in your job, and you are constantly working towards perfection. Whatever perfection might be within a standard class or job, it is very rarely defined by you; instead, it is defined by a parent, a teacher, an employer, or somebody else. Schools operate as they do because, in order to keep the machines running, most of us need to be employees, and most of us need to work towards perfection. Even as an entrepreneur, you will likely want your employees to work towards perfection, in most cases, as much as possible, and within reason.

Problems arise when you try to break out of that systemic mold, and say, "Wait a second. I don't want to be part of this conveyor belt. I want to create my own system. I want to do my own things. In fact, I want to do it completely differently." Problems arise when you try to break free from the conveyor belt methodology that has been ingrained inside your brain since the age of five. You are fighting against something that has been programmed into your very being, against your very nature, for years and years and years. If you try to fight against that grain and against that training, you are going to struggle. Instead, retrain your brain.

I believe that this is at the core of why so many businesses fail. Instead of successfully changing their mindset, these prospective entrepreneurs continue to try to fight against what they have been taught their entire lives, or they don't know enough to change it. They strive for perfection as they have been trained to do, never reaching it, and never moving forward.

Now that you understand how your mind has been trained and how your drive for perfection was born, you can start to identify your thought patterns. You can start to identify your ways of thinking and how you can start to change that thinking. By changing your mindset, you can truly set yourself, and your business, free.

CHAPTER FOUR

Perfectionism in Thoughts

In this chapter I am going to explore perfectionism in the way that you think and in the very thoughts that you have inside your head. As I addressed in the previous chapter, your brain has been trained to focus on perfectionism from a very young age. If you don't actively work to reverse what has been instilled within you for so long, you will inevitably succumb to it. We need to train our brains to form new habits and new pathways in order to achieve more. This is true whether you are working on something big or small, as it is hard to resist what you have been trained to do.

You must change the very way your subconscious mind informs and persuades your conscious mind. This is much simpler said than done; however, it can be achieved if you put your mind to it, pun intended. The way you think affects how you act, what you do, and which decisions you make. You must stamp out this corruption of your thought patterns if you are to have any chance of success. All action stems from a thought. Therefore, in order to achieve success, all thoughts must be controlled and redirected appropriately along their path.

The first step in this corrective process is to identify which of your thoughts are contributing to your pursuit of perfection. Here are some examples of perfectionists' thoughts:

1. *What if they don't like it?*
2. *What if it's missing something?*
3. *What if they return it because…?*
4. *We can't be seen like that. (Please note that this statement can have merit but not often.)*
5. *If we can just finish this one last thing, we can put it out there and be done with it.*
6. *Just a few more tweaks and I'll finally be done.*
7. *It won't take me to long to make this change.*
8. *I can finish it quickly if I can just get this one piece done.*
9. *We can add these few minor things.*

Now, these are just some quick examples of what perfectionists may think. The phrasing and terminology that you use in your own head will likely be different. However, if you find yourself saying or thinking variations of these statements, you definitely have a mindset issue that you need to overcome. Unfortunately, for a true perfectionist, it may be easy to rationalize these thoughts. You may even be tempted to think that your own statements are different enough or that your situation is different enough that this list is not applicable to you. If you find yourself thinking this, then you are deeper into the fixed perfectionist mindset than you realize. Your brain will try every trick it can to prevent you from changing. Instead of just reading the list as it is written, consider how you personally think these thoughts and how you personally say these statements. There may be subtle differences, but the harm these words cause is the same.

Consider the list again. The underlying message in each of these thoughts is the same: always compare yourself against something or someone else, and let outside forces determine whether or not you are done and whether or not you are okay to continue.

This message is a major part of the problem. Only you, as the owner of your business, can determine if something is done or not done. Now, certainly your customers and other folks might have feedback. However, at the end of the day, it is your business, and it is your right to decide when something is or is not good enough. Keep an eye out for these kinds of thoughts, and stamp them out whenever possible, not only in yourself, but possibly also in your team as well.

Now, you will want to use some caution here. As I noted before, there are times when these thoughts might be justified and when having these thoughts might actually make sense. Therefore, whatever it is that you are working on, whenever it is that you are having these thoughts, remember the 80/20 rule, and ask yourself, "Are these thoughts occurring in the 80% portion, or are they occurring in the 20% portion?"

Only you can decide if your thoughts are justified while they are occurring. Only you can decide when it is okay to push forward and when you are holding yourself back. Only you can decide into which category those thoughts fall during whichever particular project you are working on. However, knowing what to keep an eye out for, you can start identifying these thoughts while they are happening and make more informed decisions about how to address them.

This process of self-policing your own mind will likely be the hardest step in beating perfectionism. Because these thoughts are ingrained, because they are so deeply seated within your mind, they are not going to suddenly disappear overnight. It will take continuous and constant practice identifying your thoughts in order to address and change them.

I challenge you to start right now. Are you with me? How many of you, after reading my challenge, thought, "Well, this is ridiculous. There is no possible way I can do that." There. Right there is your first perfectionist thought, and it is in need of addressing. You are thinking that you are not good enough or that you cannot change these thoughts. *That* is the antithesis of the fixed perfectionist mindset. Keep looking out for this and great things will start happening. You will notice yourself, and your thoughts, changing.

Most of the time, if you are stuck in a fixed perfectionist mindset, these thoughts will just happen. They will simply appear in your mind as though they are a part of your being. I want you to realize that they are not a part of your being, but they have been a part of your training and your conditioning. Once you remember that these thoughts are not a part of who you are at your core, it will become significantly easier for you to change these thoughts. Know that training and conditioning can be changed. Accepting that this is possible is a key step in changing a fixed perfectionist mindset to a growth entrepreneur mindset.

Whenever you find yourself having these thoughts, you need to stop whatever you are doing, stop your mind from thinking any further, and say, "Wait. Why did I just think that? Does it actually make sense right now, or am I just applying my fear of not being perfect to what I am doing? Can I move forward with this? Have I achieved the DBP line or not?"

There is no doubt that it will be hard, but as you practice these steps, you will form new thought patterns in your brain, and it will become easier and easier and easier.

Here are three great ways to help you identify perfectionist thoughts and drive them away:

1. *Encourage your team members to call each other out.*

When someone from your team notices that you are thinking or saying perfection driven statements, they should immediately interrupt you and call you out on it. Stop yourself, and tell your mind, "This thought is NOT okay. Instead, I could have said...." and complete that sentence with a more positive "get things done" type of thought. This will help retrain your brain.

Of course, this can be a recipe for disaster if there aren't some proper ground rules set in place. Here are some rules that I recommend:

a. *You must be willing to take it.*

You must accept this criticism knowing that you are a work in progress and that the team is only trying to help you out. They are helping you out of the good of their hearts, so that your business can grow faster, because they respect who you are, what you do, and what you have done for them.

b. *Everyone is equal during mindset training.*

No one on the team should be fearful of calling out their boss, or anyone in the company, while they are having perfectionist thoughts. It should not come across as a reprimand; instead, it should be seen as an opportunity for growth. In setting this rule, no one can reprimand or hold someone negatively accountable for saying these things, so your team is free to open up and address perfectionism when it arises. Only when you are free from reprimand and repercussion can you really start to see growth in this process. It should also not be a vindictive process. The goal is not to make someone feel like he or she messed up. The goal is the mutual growth of the team.

c. *Create an Interrupt Word*

I have found it is best to use a simple word, or a short set of words, that would not normally be found in conversation, as an acceptable word for triggering an interruption. This word can be blurted out when someone hears a fixed perfectionist statement. The interruption will help your brain start to form new growth entrepreneur connections instead of reinforcing the fixed perfectionist thought patterns. This is yet another step towards taking your thoughts out of the danger zone and into a safe zone. Accept suggestions from your team while defining this word. Every business is different, every area of expertise is different, and what everyone is working on within a business will be different. The more the word means to the team, the quicker it will help everyone overcome perfectionism. It should not be just any word that Bob McIntosh said you should use in some book you read. It should be a word defined by you and your team to give it significantly more meaning, and, as a result, it will be taken much more seriously.

2. **Start to identify these thoughts and drive them away.**

Have checkpoints set up in everything you do. These checkpoints will help you determine when you are stuck trying to make something perfect or if you are on track and getting things done.

When you reach a checkpoint, take a conscious step back to evaluate what you are working on. It doesn't matter what it is, whether it is a small piece of a big project, a big project for the whole company, or just the company itself. If you are unsure of whether you are stuck or on track, it may help to bring in another team member to provide a different perspective. This outside perspective can often tip the scales one way or another.

Evaluate what you are working on. Evaluate everything that you are going through and where it is in relation to the end goal of the project. If you realize you have passed the DBP line, you need to stop, wrap-up what you are working on, and move forward.

Only by introducing these mental checkpoints in which you stop yourself and ask, "Am I stuck in a pattern of perfection?" can you start to identify when perfectionist thoughts are occurring. Identifying them will become easier with practice. Before long, you will be doing it naturally, without prompting, and when that happens, you will know you have successfully changed your mindset. Your mind will automatically start changing to create these new positive and habitual thought processes when you begin applying them continually.

3. Seek out a mentor, or several mentors, to help you along the way.

Having a mentor, or group of mentors, you can trust with private information about your business is critical. A great mentor can offer experience and perspective when it comes to perfectionism in your business. Think of mentors as your own personal board of advisors.

I have several great mentors who have helped me grow tremendously, especially when I was just getting started, not only as a business owner, but also as a person. I can't recommend this enough. Great mentors are invaluable to your business. They will also be a great sounding board when you are stuck on a project.

I do want to take a moment to talk about mentors and coaches. I believe there is a difference between the two, and it is important to note. A coach is someone you pay to help you achieve a specific goal. This person is skilled in the area or niche in which you require assistance. A mentor is someone who can provide perspective on what you are working on. They are often not paid, and your relationship is not defined by the accomplishment of an end goal. A good entrepreneur will have both mentors and coaches to help them in their business.

If you get to one of your mental checkpoints, and you are truly stuck, unable to decide where you are on your path, a mentor can come into play to advise you. I would only seek out this mentor if you don't have a team member who is educated enough in the project to provide an informed opinion. Mentors are not there to hold your hand, but mentors can show you the path. Be sure to respect your mentor's time, and don't contact them constantly, lest you ruin the relationship.

If you don't have a mentor yet, I highly recommend that you go out and seek one. They don't necessarily have to be in your specific niche or in the same business. In fact, it will often be best if they are not in your same business. Instead, find someone who knows business and knows how to grow a business. Find a mentor who is where you want to be, and who has achieved what you want to achieve. If your mentor has already achieved what you want to achieve, he or she will be much more likely to give you advice that will help you get to where you ultimately want to be.

I have provided three great ways to help you along with the process. As you fight the good fight, you might discover others. I encourage you to use whatever methods you find, even if they aren't listed here. In fact, I encourage you to share what you do find, especially if you find other great methods for helping to identify perfectionist thought patterns.

You can share them on our Facebook page *www.facebook.com/donebp*. When we combine our knowledge, we learn and grow exponentially faster!

We are always looking to find the best possible way to interrupt these negative thought patterns of perfection and start to improve ourselves. Many of you are extremely creative. In fact, you wouldn't be an entrepreneur if you didn't have at least some creativity in your mind, so I am excited to see what you, my readers, come up with for interrupting your thought patterns.

Over time, your thoughts will change, and your actions will start to follow your thoughts. Just remember to be constantly improving and battling the perfectionism that has been ingrained in your mind since you were very young. One day, suddenly, you will realize that you have indeed changed. You will simply wake up one day and realize your mindset has shifted. It won't be a sudden off-the-cliff type of shift. It will occur in small steps, so after giving it some time, stop for a second, and realize how many small steps you have taken. Turn around, and you will see that you are most of the way up the mountain of success already.

Now, you have identified your brain patterns, you have learned how to fight your negative perfectionist thoughts, and you have started to identify ways to fix those brain patterns and thoughts. You can move forward with confidence.

CHAPTER FIVE

Excellence Over Perfection

In business, all too often, you will find yourself striving for perfection rather than looking for excellence. When I talk about applying the concepts of this book to your life, I don't mean to say that excellence is a pattern of perfection. In fact, more often than not, you can have an excellent business that isn't perfect or a perfect business that isn't excellent. A great example of this is the iPhone from Apple. Every new generation of iPhone is followed by the inevitable critique, "It would be perfect, if only it had xyz feature." Apple certainly knew about these features and knew that including them would make the phone perfect. However, they also knew if they delivered a product that wasn't excellent, the phone would suffer a far worse fate. Realizing that excellence is a better indicator of success than perfection will help you change how you perceive your business. After all, I think we can agree that though the iPhone is not perfect, it has been a massive success. Acknowledging this will help you change how you approach your business.

Let's first define excellence as the quality of being outstanding or extremely good, whereas we define perfection as the condition or state or quality of being free, or nearly free, from flaws and defects. Notice the difference between the two. Excellence does not mean perfection, and perfection doesn't necessarily mean excellence.

When you are looking at your business, you should strive for excellence. If you can successfully achieve excellence in your business, your customers and the people who work with you will recognize that excellence, and they will be attracted to that excellence.

People are willing to overlook a lack of perfection if the end product is still excellent. Though it may not be perfect, it can still be extremely good; therefore, people will still be satisfied, and that is what you should be striving for. You want to strive for excellence over perfection.

In order to strive for excellence, you need to understand who determines what that excellence is, both in and for your business.

Identify those people. Generally speaking, excellence is determined and defined by the following groups of people:

1. It is defined by your customers.
2. It is defined by your peers.
3. It is defined by your competitors.
4. It is defined by your employees.

These are the folks who define excellence. Notice that excellence is *not* defined by you; however, perfection is the exact opposite. Perfection is *not* defined by your customers. It is *not* defined by your peers. It is *not* defined by your competitors, and it is *not* defined by your employees. Perfection is, by default, defined by you, for only you can say if something is perfect or free from flaws or defects within your business. Where you see a flaw, someone else might see perfection. Whereas you may see a defect, someone else may say that if the supposed defect doesn't hinder the progress of what needs to be done, it is perfect!

This is the difference between perfection and excellence, and this is why you should always be striving for excellence. A good business needs customers, good peer reviews, and good employees. A good business will likely have competitors as well. All of these folks will help define excellence, because these are the folks that really matter when it comes to your business.

If you are constantly trying to live up to your own standards, which are moving targets, you are always going to be let down. Part of what makes you a great entrepreneur is that your standards will always be higher than other people's standards, even if those standards don't necessarily make sense. If you didn't have a higher level of standard, you would not have been likely to create your own business. If you had lower standards, you would have been content with a 9 to 5 type of job, wherein your life would have consisted of punching the clock, confined and defined by what you earn at that job.

This is not who you are as entrepreneur. You started your businesses to change your life, to change what you do, and to change your state. The only reason that you need to change currently is because you are not satisfied by what you currently have. You see more for yourself. You see more for somebody else. You see more in everything that you do, and it is for this reason that nothing will ever be perfect. Perfect is impossible for you to achieve; it is a constantly moving target.

Let's say you have a very successful business. Well, that is great, but I would be willing to bet that even though you have a very successful business, you still wish it were even more successful. (If not, then you probably don't need to keep reading this book!) My guess is also that if you started this business yourself, you didn't necessarily say to yourself that where you are now was the perfect end goal. Your first goal may have been that you wanted to make your first million dollars. Then, once you reached that goal, it morphed into wanting to make your first $10 million. Once you have achieved that goal, you will find that your goal will have changed into yet another target. That goal is perfection. No matter how much you want it, and no matter how much you think you have defined it, it will never be achieved because it is always a moving target.

Perfection for customers, peers, competitors, and employees is defined as excellence. These folks are not looking for things to be perfect. They are looking to have an excellent experience, an excellent result, a range of excellent products to purchase, or whatever else it might be that they want, and they want it to be as top-notch as possible.

Customers are people, and they know, as people, that nothing is ever perfect. There might be brief moments of perfection, but they never last. Therefore, customers don't go to a business expecting it to be 100% perfect, but they *do* go to businesses expecting that business to deliver excellence in whatever it is that they are doing and offering. Strive for excellence in your business.

Here is a list of ways through which you can strive for excellence in your own business:

1. Identify your core values.

These are the things that truly matter in your company. Everyone who works for or with you should know what these values are. They should resonate with you as a person, and they should reflect what you want your company to be. Most importantly, they should be defined by you, the entrepreneur.

I certainly encourage you to take input from your employees if you have them, your mentors, or from anyone else you work with on your team. However, at the end of the day, the core values of your business must be defined by you, and they should directly reflect what you believe and how you operate.

These values are what every single team member, employee, contractor, or anyone else should follow, and they should believe in these values. By having people on your team who have the same core values as you, you set yourself up for a much higher level of excellence in everything that you do. One of my mentors calls this having a "code of honor" for your team, a code your team will not just follow but also believe in and truly live, both at work and outside of work. Excellence needs a structure to be supported and your core values can provide the necessary structure.

2. Define your mission.

By defining your mission, you help your team understand what your end goal is. Your definition may be in the form of an official mission statement or a simple phrase or sentence you have jotted down. No matter what form it takes, have a mission, and make sure that everyone knows that mission.

Your mission may change over time, and that is fine, as long as everyone on the team is aware of those changes. When everyone is working towards the same end goal, success will happen, progress will be made, and excellence will be achieved.

3. *Truly listen.*

Listen to your customers. Listen to your peers. Listen to your competitors. Listen to your critics. Listen to people who praise you. Listen to people who hate you.

Just because you listen to them doesn't mean that you have to implement everything that they say; however, by truly listening to what they are telling you, you will be able to more easily identify where you have room for improvement and where you are absolutely killing it. Now, sometimes—in fact, many times—implementing a suggestion from a customer or peer may not make sense for your business, but if you are not listening to what your customers want, if you are not listening to what people are saying about your business, you cannot possibly ever achieve a high level of excellence.

4. *Restrain your emotions.*

Other people may let out their emotions, but as an owner of a business, you need to keep cool in all situations. This doesn't mean that you can't go out and just let loose; however, it does mean that you should not do so in front of your customers, employees, or anyone who works or deals for or with your business.

You are running a business. Getting extremely emotional about something will only complicate matters, and let's be honest, it looks very unprofessional. Emotion will reduce your ability to deliver an effective product. It will blind you to listening to the people around you. It will detract from your mission and even your core values. When emotion runs high, intelligence runs low.

I don't mean to say that you need to be a robot 100% of the time, never displaying or having any emotion at all. You are a business owner, after all, and you are likely passionate about your business. However, to achieve a high level of excellence, if you find yourself in an emotional state, step away for a few minutes, and let yourself calm down. Get your emotions in check, and then, and only then, should you tackle the issue at hand.

Remember, when emotion runs high, intelligence runs low, and when emotion runs low, intelligence runs high. Make sure you are operating your business at the highest level of intelligence, unobstructed by emotion.

5. *Journal.*

I will admit that when I first learned about journaling, I scoffed at the entire concept. It seemed pointless. Why do I need to write down my thoughts? What benefit could this possibly give me? I changed my mind when a co-worker introduced me to some of the more interesting aspects of journaling. Did you know that Richard Branson journals, reflecting upon his day, nearly every day?

When someone like Richard Branson—one of my personal business heroes and someone who is worth, at the time of this writing, roughly $6 billion—journals and feels that it has a positive effect in his life and in his business, I sit down and take notice.

After trying journaling myself, I now find it to be a useful tool. Journaling doesn't have to take a long time or add another complicated item to your day; however, it is often good to commit your thoughts to paper rather than leave them to rumble around in your head. I also find that, even though I am a computer person by default, it is better to actually put pen to paper. This isn't just my opinion. A 2010 Wall Street Journal article also addressed this point, citing the results of an Indiana University study. In this study, children who practiced printing by hand showed more "adult-like" neuro patterns. This translates to adults as well and is consistent with my own experiences. Numerous other studies have also come to similar printing-over-typing results.

Maintain an actual bound journal, and rest assured that mistakes are okay. Nobody else needs to read your journal. Let those mistakes happen. You may even find that, as your subconscious begins letting out trapped information, what you write will turn out not to be a mistake at all!

Write what comes to mind. If you write it and you don't like it, you can always cross it out, but I would recommend that you don't erase it completely. It is going to be an interesting journey, at some point in time, to walk back through your journals and read all of your ideas and plans and even those things you may have thought were mistakes.

In fact, while writing this book, I returned to a journal I started in 2012 and read some of the things I had written. In doing so, I was fascinated by the things that I wrote and how small-minded they now seem, and I was also reminded of goals I had set for myself but have yet to achieve. I realized the growth and progress I have made, and I was reminded of the areas in which I can continue to push forward. It is great to reread your thoughts and realize your own progress, even if you didn't accomplish every goal.

As you become used to the process of journaling, you will find that the practice will help you achieve a higher level of thought, and it will help you improve your mindset. If you start seeing repeated patterns of perfectionism in your entries, you may need to revisit the chapter on attacking perfectionism in your thoughts. Use your own mind to change your own mindset. Your journal will not lie to you. It offers a direct insight into your brain.

In order to make the most of this practice, I recommend that you journal at least once a day. You don't have to write pages upon pages. In fact, my journal is kept in a small, simple binder, and I usually fill a half to a full page per day. It usually only requires a few minutes of time reflecting on my thoughts for the day and writing them down.

I have also gotten into the practice of writing down the things for which I am grateful. I believe that by acknowledging my gratitude, I will gain an increasing appreciation for the things I have. I recommend you give this a try!

Journaling is a simple technique, and it does not require much of your time. Many of us lie in bed for several minutes, if not longer, thinking before falling asleep. Why not use that opportunity to write down those thoughts? Then, later on, go back and review them.

6. *Practice gratitude.*

As I mentioned in the journaling exercise, I believe it is helpful to express gratitude in your journal in order to increase your overall gratitude in life. Express gratitude towards your customers, your employees, and anyone else involved in or with your business. This is a fantastic way to improve how you feel personally, and I have yet to find someone who dislikes receiving thanks.

If you find yourself feeling down or discouraged, if you don't feel good and your mindset is very low, return to your journal and remind yourself of all the things for which you are thankful. Then, take another minute to add a few more items to that list. Do it with a smile on your face. It may seem silly, but a smile can be a very important thing.

Practicing gratitude when you wake up every morning as well as when you go to bed every night will improve your days overall. Be sure to include not just your business, but also your family, friends, and anything else in your life you are grateful for having. Nobody starts off a bad day by thinking about happy, positive things in life. In fact, if you are starting off a bad day, you can often change the tone of the day completely by pausing to acknowledge your gratitude. It is really that simple.

7. Smile!

A well timed smile can completely change the mood of a room by releasing tension. Riggio's 2012 Psychology Today post highlights that smiling can make you feel better. By spending just a few minutes a day smiling while looking at yourself in a mirror, you can completely improve your mood.

In fact, I once attended a seminar in which the keynote speaker had a room of nearly 600 people perform this profound, yet simple, exercise. We paired off with folks we had never met before, and one partner had to hold the biggest, goofiest, widest smile they possibly could for eight seconds straight. The other partner had to try to remain passive by not laughing, not giggling, and not showing any expression or emotion at all. We then reversed roles and repeated the process. Both times, more than 90% of the participants could not contain their emotion while looking at someone who was smiling at them. Keep in mind, each exercise round lasted only eight seconds. Eight simple seconds! That is not very long at all. In fact, go ahead and count off eight seconds to yourself right now. Go ahead. I'll wait.

If smiling at someone for eight seconds can change their mood, then why wouldn't you make this a standard part of your life? Why wouldn't you show the people around you that you appreciate them by smiling?

8. Learn something every day.

Set aside time each day to learn something new or to revisit something you learned in the past. Only by staying current and relevant can you hope to achieve excellence in your business.

I recommend that you spend at least 30 minutes per day focused on educating yourself. There is a wealth of amazing books you can read, online classes you can watch, seminars you can attend, simple blog posts you can peruse, and so many more learning opportunities.

By calibrating your brain to learn every single day, you will consistently grow, and you will consistently realize how much more you can accomplish. You will achieve your goals, and you will continue to set bigger, better, and bolder goals.

If you are not learning, then you are falling behind. In this day and age, everything can change in a blink of an eye. What you need to take away from this fact is that everything changes, and you must keep up. Now, I'm not saying that you need to be on top of every single little thing happening in your industry or your niche; in fact, more often than not, doing so will be impossible. However, if you spend just 30 minutes of your day focused on educating yourself about something new, such as a new method of marketing, discovering a new niche, or whatever else might develop, you will, over the course of a single year, spend 180 hours increasing your knowledge bank. That is very, very powerful.

Remember to keep your learning within a fairly rigid amount of time. You do not want to get lost in continuously learning and never actually achieving anything in your business. Set a timeframe, and stick to it. If a specific learning piece will require more time, that's fine, but try to spread it out if possible, instead of trying to complete it all at once. If you spend an entire day or more at a conference, make sure to devote additional time to your business, implementing your newly acquired knowledge, upon your return.

9.   *Teach others.*

If you have learned something from your business, don't be afraid to teach others. Not only does it feel great to help other people out, it is also a great opportunity to network and to be seen as an authority.

What many people don't realize is that as soon as you become a teacher, speaker, or group leader for the benefit of business education, you suddenly become an authority in that space, regardless of how much you know or how long you have been doing it.

Now, the number of people that you attract will ultimately determine how much of an authority you are; however, being seen as an authority will lead people to think and sometimes even say that what you are doing must be excellent due to your perceived value. As long as you are following these other methods of applying excellence in your business, you will certainly have an excellent business, achieve your goals, and allow other people to have confidence in your accomplishments.

Teaching others is a great way to not only give back and feel uplifted, but it is also a great way to grow your business and be seen as an authority on and purveyor of excellence.

10. *Ask yourself, every single day, if you have given your very best.*

If you are sincere and honest with your answer to this question, you won't be able to answer "yes" every single day. That is to be expected, and it is not a problem. However, if you find yourself saying "no" for too many days in a row, it may be time for a change. It could be a change in your tasks. It could be a change in an entire project. It could be a change in your business. It could be a change in you.

The important thing to remember is that when you find that you have not been giving your best for too many days in a row, you need to sit down and evaluate why that is and what you need to do to get back on track.

Even if you only implement 50% of these ten items discussed—just five items—you will still far outshine many other folks in your niche. Now, imagine what would happen if you did all ten of them; imagine what levels of excellence your business could achieve by simply applying all of these things every single day. Imagine where your business would, and could, be.

As I close out this chapter on learning and striving for excellence over perfection, I want to leave you with this: excellence is defined by your customers, peers, and external third parties sources, but perfection is defined by you. When you are looking at your business, take into account what "they" think more than what you think. External determiners are always more important.

CHAPTER SIX

Get Out Of Your Own Way In Business

This is the big question: How can you achieve the results you want to achieve in your business?

For many of you, applying the DBP philosophy will require a complete change from your current practices. For others, whose practices are already very similar to DBP, it will require only a simple sidestep. No matter how different or similar your practices may be, making changes, even simple ones, can seem overwhelming. Let this chapter be your step-by-step guide. By breaking down the transformation process, you will be better able to adopt and apply the DBP philosophy to your business. This will be your awakening moment as you begin to realize just how fluidly and easily you can embrace Done is Better than Perfect.

As you work through this chapter, you will begin exploring the many different areas and aspects of business to which DBP can be applied. Not all of these aspects will apply to every single business because every business is unique. However, the foundational ideas and concepts addressed through each area and aspect, regardless of the illustrated size, longevity, or niche, will hold true.

Selling products or services

Most entrepreneurs start out by selling a range of products or services. They begin by selecting products and services they have the most experience with, because they are usually the easiest to get started due to their existing knowledge of said product or service, yet all too often, these entrepreneurs fail. Why? They were waiting for perfection.

You will never ever launch your product or service successfully if you wait for it to be perfect. By waiting for it to be perfect, you are simply setting yourself up for failure. Failure could come in the form of competitors. They may hear about your idea and decide that it's a great one. If they launch it before you do, it could lead to failure. Failure could also come in the form of procrastination. You may never actually launch your amazing idea because you just keep continuing to test it and tweak it, and test it and tweak it. Instead of launching a successful business, you will end up launching nothing more than a time-consuming hobby.

Time is the ultimate enemy of an entrepreneur; you can't afford to waste a single moment of it. Remember your 80/20 rule, get your product or service running, and send it out into the market. The 20% that isn't yet complete, the part for which you are striving for perfection, will be okay remaining unfinished or imperfect. A "perfect" product or service will almost never result in additional sales of any significance. Sure, you might get a few added sales, but if you never actually release your product, you won't have any sales at all. I would rather earn 80% of some sales than 100% of no sales.

Remember, you can almost always go back and tweak or update the product or service later on. You can almost always add things you have missed or fix things you need to improve. In fact, you will often find that, once you have launched, the things that may indeed need to be fixed won't be the same things you anticipated fixing, and the things you were sure would need to be improved won't be the things your customers care about anyway. Most of the time, you are going to realize that your product or service is fine just the way it already is. The excellence of your product or service is primarily defined by your customers. Let them tell you if and where you can improve.

It is rare for something to be so overwhelmingly bad that you won't be able to fix it and repair any damage done. You are an entrepreneur, and a risk taker by default. Launching your product is just one more risk that you must take in order to be successful. Don't fret about the fact that it's not 100% perfect. It likely never will be. Instead, put it out there and work with it. Try it out. Test it. See what happens. Take any feedback you receive and make modifications, and then put it back out there again.

Now, for physical products specifically, you will often have stricter Done is Better than Perfect lines in place than for services or digitally delivered products. Physical products require a lot more time, effort, and money upfront in order to make them happen. In many cases when you are producing a physical product, there will be laws and regulations to which you must adhere. Take these laws and regulations into account. Getting something done only to have it shut down or nullified by the government would be counterproductive. Following these laws and regulations should always be considered part of your 80% when getting something done.

Perhaps you are offering both a product and a service. In most cases, the service can be launched much sooner than the product can be launched. Digitally delivered products, like e-books, membership sites, or other things that can be more easily changed and modified can also have shorter time tables and usually have very few laws or regulations restricting their production and sale.

No matter what you are selling, whether it is a product or a service, don't wait for it to be perfect. Put it out there as quickly as possible, in order to make sales as quickly as possible. No matter what your reasons and motivations for starting your business, if your business doesn't make any money, your reasons and motivations will be irrelevant. If you aren't generating income, your business simply will not continue to run, unless you have an endless supply of cash, and most of us do not. You must focus on earning income, and that means you must focus on launching your product or service. Only when your business has begun earning money can you begin to achieve the things you want to achieve. Only with money can you have the freedom of time, the freedom of choice, and the other freedoms your business was meant to help you achieve.

Marketing campaigns

Marketing is the lifeblood of all companies, and just as it is the case with products and services, it is better to release a marketing plan than is not quite perfect than to wait and lose potential customers. Without marketing or a marketing plan, your business will often fail before ever having a chance to start. If you don't attract customers, it won't matter how much time and money you spend on other aspects of your business. Keep in mind that even though companies like TOMS shoes did not execute a specific marketing campaign and relied instead on word of mouth, which can work if your product lends itself to that, these companies still had a marketing plan in place.

Most of your time—80% of your time—should be spent on revenue generating activities. The foundation of those activities should be marketing. If you're not marketing, then you're not going to survive. You may be lucky, but it is always better to create your own luck than to rely on somebody else's.

When I talk about Done is Better than Perfect in relation to marketing, the biggest hang-ups for most entrepreneurs are spelling and grammar. Instead of getting stuck on punctuation errors, commas getting confused with semi-colons, colons getting confused with periods, and misspellings, realize that more often than not, these mistakes are very minor. In most cases, word processing programs will get you close enough to be able to consider a project done. If you are constantly stressing out over spelling and grammar, then you are going to be using up your focus on details that are not nearly as important as the actual content of your campaign.

Whether or not a comma is misplaced is not going to make or break your business. Whether or not a semi-colon or a period is supposed to be used is not going to allow you to generate more revenue. Focus on the right things—the important things—for your business, and realize that minor and generally insignificant details can always be fixed later on.

With that said, you should obviously not put out a marketing piece that is completely riddled with mistakes, but you also don't have to spend 80% of your time going back and looking over every little misspelling, punctuation mark, or grammatical error. These things are often not worth your time. If you are truly irked by them,

I recommend you hire someone who can help you, so you can focus your time on true revenue generating activities.

Focus instead on getting your message heard and getting it in front of as many eyeballs as possible. Even if your message is not the best one out there, at least it will be heard by an audience. You can always fine tune and tweak your message in order to make it better before going any further with it, but if no one ever sees it, no one is ever going to act on it either. In fact, one of the best strategies I have used in several of my businesses was to recruit early adopters into the business, knowing full well that these early adopters won't care as much about mistakes and they will the opportunity to use the product or service early. Early adopters will teach you invaluable information you can use to tweak marketing and services and increase effectiveness.

Realize as well that in today's day and age, marketing, and fine tuning and tweaking your message, is now easier than ever with the advent of Google AdWords, pay per click services, Facebook ads, and many other online advertisement services. If you find an error, you can simply access your ad and fix it. You don't have to stew over it for extended periods of time prior to its release. Sure, you might lose a customer here or there due to spelling or grammar mistakes, but I would rather lose one or two customers for minor reasons than never have any customers because the ad remained on my desk.

Most entrepreneurs that I have taught or consulted with struggle the most with this aspect of marketing. Marketing is the first thing their potential customers see, and they want it to be perfect in order to make the best possible impression. Their drive for perfection is especially heightened when it comes to the written word, and they spend too much time striving to achieve that perfection. In order to avoid this trap, you should set yourself a deadline for any marketing activities. If that set date comes and goes and you are still working on that activity, take a step back and consider why.

Remember those checkpoints I addressed previously? This is a great opportunity to implement one. Once you hit your checkpoint, stop and ask yourself if your task at hand is done or not. If you are being sincere and honest with yourself, and if it's really not done, then continue working. There are times when deadlines just don't work out, or when the project has morphed into something more and requires additional time, and that's okay. However, if you look at your work and say, "It's not perfect, but it will work," then put it out there. If, later on, you find that it needs tweaking, then change it as you move forward. This is a great way to achieve more success in your business.

Finishing anything

I have explained how you can apply Done is Better than Perfect to selling products and services and working on your marketing campaigns, but you can really apply this concept to *anything* in your business. Perhaps it is a project you've been developing. Perhaps it is your financial reporting. It could be anything, really; what it is isn't what's important. What *is* important is that you get things done.

Here are a few questions you can ask yourself in order to help you get something, anything, done:

1. *Have you provided enough to make it work or to make it understandable and usable?*

If you have, then you can move to on to the next question. Again, take into consideration any laws or regulations before answering this question. If you have not, then keep working until you can answer, "Yes."

2. *How much time have you spent to get to this point, and how much more time will it take you to get to the 100% perfect point?*

Consider the 80/20 rule before answering. It will likely take you 20% of the time to get 80% of the way to perfect. Are you at that 80% mark? If so, consider wrapping up whatever is still open and calling this thing done. Can you add the remaining 20% later on? Will it be functional or usable without that 20%? If you can answer affirmatively to either or both of these questions, then you are ready to move on to the third question.

3. *Can you accept that you are done? Are you confident in your work?*

This should be the easiest question to address; however, for many, it will be the most difficult. Simply accept that you are done, and let yourself move on to the next project, marketing activity, product, or whatever your "next" will be. Move on, knowing you are confident that what you have done is done, even though it isn't perfect. Remember, you can always return to modify, tweak, update, or change it later on.

These three simple questions can be applied to any project, any business, any industry, any niche, anywhere. If you ask yourself these questions, and if you answer them honestly, you will start to see increasing success in your business.

Business start-ups

Lately, there have been a large number of start-ups, especially in technology based industries. Many of these start-ups fail simply because they lack the ability to get things done. How can you apply DBP to a start-up, whether it be in a tech industry or any other industry?

Here are a few simple things to keep in mind:

1. *You only get one chance to launch something, but you can always rebrand it, and re-launch it, if you need to.*

Realize that people love updates to products and services. It lets them know that you are constantly improving the product or the service. Updating makes people feel like you care more about what you are providing. This increases perceived value, which will make your customers more likely to become long-term customers of your business.

This may seem contrary to the popular belief that a product must be perfect for customers to want to buy it, but remember, if you are constantly striving for excellence, what you put out will be excellent, even if it's not perfect. Think about cell phones, especially the smart phone market. The major smart phone players, Samsung and Apple, are constantly releasing new phones with new features. People aren't upset that the phone they originally bought didn't have those new features; rather, they are excited at the opportunity to upgrade to a new and improved model of their phone! If it is excellent, and then you make it even better down the road, imagine how positive its reception will be. (Apple does a phenomenal job of this with their iPhone line.) Imagine its power on your customers. Imagine what they will think about your business *now*.

2. *Most new companies fail from sitting still for too long.*

Keep moving forward no matter what. Here are a couple of ideas to help you do just that:

- If you find yourself sitting still over a period of time, figure out what is keeping you from moving forward. Again, checkpoints can be implemented to act as boosters in order to help push you forward faster.
- Identify your road block, and then identify how to remove it. More often than not, you will find that there is just one small thing pausing your business. One little pebble in a gear will completely stop a machine, but once that little pebble has been removed, everything will continue moving forward without issue. Find that

pebble and eliminate it ruthlessly. Plus, moving forward just feels good!

Asking yourself the following questions can also help unstick your business:

✓ *Will what I have right now achieve my desired end result or experience I want my customers to have?*

If the answer is "yes," then you are done! Great! If the answer is "no," then keep on working.

✓ *What is the worst thing that will happen if I go with what I have right now? What is the best thing that will happen if I go with what I have right now?*

Realize that the worst thing you can imagine will almost never occur. Much like our high school selves, worrying about all the possible negative reactions to asking someone on a date, we create these fantastical and imaginary situations that will never ever occur. For many of you, this same defeatist attitude is still holding you back. The worst thing that could happen is very unlikely. Now, the reason I also have you consider the best possible result is because I want you to imagine. Imagine what it would feel like if the best thing *did* happen. Instead of always focusing on the negative, make sure you spend an equal or greater amount of time focusing on the positive. What would it feel like to have that best possible situation? What would it make you think? Where would it take your business? How would it feel to have that level of accomplishment, pride, and joy in what you are doing? I will bet in almost all cases that feeling is going to be much more powerful than the resulting feeling of the worst outcome, especially because the worst thing that could happen probably won't. Cling to that positive energy, and run with it as far as you possibly can. It will help you get more done.

✓ *If I release what I have now, can I change it later?*

The answer to this question is almost always yes. It is very rare that something cannot be updated, changed, or modified later on. Feel secure that nothing will be set in stone and unable to be changed. You have the ability to make changes should you find the need to do so.

If what you are doing does fall into one of those rare times in which things really can't be changed later on, or if making a change could result in long term delays due to regulatory or legal concerns, then you need to make sure that you are truly done. Take a step back to evaluate where you are right now. If you truly need perfection, then keep working towards it. There are certainly instances when this is true; however, those instances are the exception and not the rule.

The Team

As an entrepreneur, no matter what, you will need a team to be successful. You will need others to help you. You cannot possibly achieve any major level of success on your own.

This doesn't mean that your team has to be tens of thousands of employees in every single country in the world, but it does mean that you need to have others surrounding and supporting you. I know plenty of very successful entrepreneurs who have eight figure businesses with only a handful of people on their team, but they still have a team. No matter what, there are times when you are going to need somebody. Just make sure that whoever that somebody is, he or she is the right person with the right mindset.

If you are running a start-up with employees or partners, or if you are running any business with employees, they will also need to learn at least the foundational tenets of Done is Better than Perfect. Take them through the steps that you have also gone through and that you think will be beneficial for them to embody.

One simple way to enhance your team's ability to avoid the traps of perfectionism is to implement spending thresholds. When you are starting a new business, there is just about a million things to be done. You won't always have the time to directly assist your team and determine when things are done. Implementing a spending threshold will help set limitations to team-led decisions. Determine a specific amount of money that you are comfortable with, and allow your team to decide what's going to happen, which direction they will go, and what the process will be, up to that amount.

For many businesses, this threshold will be around $500. If trying out a new marketing campaign is going to cost less than $500, let your team call that shot and handle it. If the campaign fails, it's not going to break your business. If it works, think about the positive effects it could have. If it works really well, then the sky's the limit!

Setting a threshold for your team allows them to operate with autonomy, which gives them a sense of freedom. When your team feels free, they are going to strive to achieve better results. You are going to find that freedom is highly invigorating for employees, and you can breathe easy knowing your business is protected by the threshold you have set. It's a win-win situation.

Now, if you find that your employees are constantly making the wrong decisions, you don't necessarily need to change the dollar threshold, but you should change their mindset. Help them understand why the decisions they made in the past were bad and how they can start making the right decisions in the future.

By implementing this practice, you are going to reach higher quality results than you ever thought possible because employees like to know they have the freedom to do what they need to do without having to work through the bureaucracy.

The more you apply Done is Better than Perfect and Get Out of Your Own Way, the more success you are going to have. Keep in mind that these simple strategies are a great starting point, but they are just that. Don't be afraid to have your team think of other ways they can apply DBP within your business. Every business will develop its own unique methodology, so let the process run its natural course. No matter what, always encourage everyone on your team, including yourself, to have the best mindset you can possibly have.

CHAPTER SEVEN

Get Out Of Your Own Way In Life

No matter what, as an entrepreneur, your time is always your most valuable resource, and it is the only resource you can never get back. As such, you need be greedy with your time, whether it is being spent on your business or within your own personal life.

There are many things within your life to which you can create simple changes in order to maximize your time. You can choose to spend that time with your family, with your friends, in your business, or with whoever and wherever. No matter how you choose to spend your time, the point remains that you will have a choice, and you will not be stuck. The more time you have, the more success you will ultimately have and the faster you will achieve it. The DBP philosophy will help you to achieve more time, so you can get on track for success.

There are several time-killing tasks within your daily life activities and within your home. You probably often find yourself working on cleaning, cooking, and laundry, for example. However, if you start applying Done is Better than Perfect to these common household chores, you will often find that you have a lot more time on your hands for devoting to your family, friends, or business.

I am going to walk you through some tasks that can easily be outsourced to save time. Now, for some of you, these tasks are stress relievers or easy time and activities you can spend with your children. If you fall into one of those categories or something similar then feel free to disregard that specific outsourcing recommendation. However, if you do not, then check out some of the amazing ways technology and modern living can help us free up our time.

1. Cleaning

This is one chore that very few people enjoy doing, and it is, therefore, one of the easiest chores to outsource. Some of you are self-proclaimed neat freaks or are in the loves-to-clean minority;

however, even if this is the case, remember that your time is your most precious resource, and it is not one to be used unnecessarily. Hiring a cleaning crew may not get your house up to your usual standards, but the fact that you are not doing it yourself means that you can spend that time growing your business.

2. Cooking

I know plenty of people who just cannot cook. In fact, my own father falls into this category. More often than not, if he is left on his own, he will either end up cooking frozen dinners—that's about the only thing that he knows how to "cook"—or eating out.

Cooking is one of those areas in which you can save a lot of time. Think about cooking and what it actually entails in terms of time. It's not just the cooking that takes up your time; it is also the driving time, the grocery buying time, the aisle walking and line-fighting time, and it is the pantry organizing time and the meal preparation time. All of the time required adds up quickly.

Let's say that the average shopping trip takes you one hour, including every aspect of that trip, even though in reality it is likely even longer. If you were to do one shopping trip just once per week, over the course of a year, you would spend 52 hours of your time on this single required component of cooking. Those 52 hours equate to over an entire week worth of business hours during which you could have been doing something beneficial and goal-oriented, whether in your business or with your family.

Going out to restaurants may seem like a viable, though pricier and often less healthy, alternative to cooking yourself. While this can be one time-saving option, because you won't have to spend as much time on all of the preparation aspects of cooking, you still have to spend time going to the restaurant, waiting to be seated at a table and for the wait staff to assist you, waiting for the restaurant to prepare food for you, eating the food, and journeying home again.

Eating out is, more often than not, an inefficient method for gaining more time, especially for startup entrepreneurs on bootstrap budgets.

The best way to save time here is to have someone shop and cook for you. You can hire people to bring you groceries, or you can simply go online and order groceries to be delivered directly to your door. There are numerous services that do this, and many grocery stores now offer a delivery service as well. Once you have your groceries, you can hire someone to come into your kitchen, use your cookware and appliances, and cook food for you. You can have a cook come once per week to create pre-portioned meals that are fridge and freezer ready. All you will have to do is warm them up. This is a great option. You will save time when compared to cooking yourself, you will save money when compared to eating at restaurants, and you can enjoy some world-class meals right in the comfort of your own home!

Imagine if you could save 52 hours a year on grocery shopping, which doesn't even include all the addition time you will save by not having to prepare and cook the food. That gained time can be well spent on your business, with your family, with your friends, or however else you want to spend it!

3. Clothing

The internet is a beautiful thing. Some companies are even starting to help with your shopping. Based on a simple conversation over the phone determining your style, how you wish to dress, and how you want to feel, these companies will send you selected clothing to meet those discussed desires and needs. Sometimes the clothing selection process is as simple as completing an online questionnaire. There are many "personal shopper" companies available to you, and they take little time to use. Typically, on a monthly basis, after determining your clothing needs, these companies will ship you clothes that are already sized and styled to fit you personally.

Shopping for clothing and trying to figure out if you are in fashion or dressed appropriately can be extremely time consuming. You no longer need to worry about that time. Clothing delivery services help you avoid having to go to the store to try on five different pairs of pants that don't fit well. You can avoid mall madness, pushy sales people, confined dressing rooms, and all the hassles that go along with shopping for yourself, by outsourcing that job.

Shopping services range in price, from as little as $60 to as much as $300-$400 for a once per month package delivery, depending on the type and quality of the desired and selected clothing. These companies are happy to help you take care of your appearance and regain your time.

4. Driving

Public transportation and apps like Uber, Sidecar, and Lift, have made driving a thing of the past for many people, especially people who live or work in big cities with major traffic issues. I have found that, often, people would fine it nice to have someone else drive them around. Wouldn't you? With another person driving, you can continue working on or preparing for meetings and presentations en route and reduce wasted time behind the wheel.

It used to be that, in order to have a driver, you would have to spend tens of thousands of dollars a year employing your own personal driver. However, apps have made it extremely inexpensive to not only have a driver, but to make it easy to get those drivers to your door, when you need them, any time, day or night. In fact, right now in Los Angeles, if I look at the Uber app, I can see that there are 15 cars within a two minute drive from where I live, who would all be willing to drive me to wherever I want to go in Los Angeles. All I have to do is tap a button, and they will be on their way to pick me up in no time. There are also numerous public transit options that run 24/7 or close to it!

Imagine what you could do with a hands-free commute, especially in a high traffic area. Let's say you are driving somewhere, and it's going to take 45 minutes. That is 45 minutes of time that you could be spending on your laptop, on a phone call, preparing for a speech, or even in a meeting. Hiring drivers offers a fantastic opportunity to save a lot of time by maximizing useable hours and reducing wasted hours.

5. Vacations and Family Time

The biggest time suck for most families is vacation. Now, I don't mean vacation in terms of going on the actual vacation, as I absolutely recommend you take as many vacations as you see fit for the benefit of both you and your family. However, did you know that most people spend more time planning a vacation than they spend planning their life, finances, and business combined? This is a mind blowing fact when you really think about it. After all, a vacation will last for one week, two weeks, or maybe even a few months for some of you, but your finances, your life, and your business will remain relevant for the rest of your life, even after your retirement.

Vacation is an area that you can absolutely have other people help you with in order to make better use of your time. There are numerous dedicated travel agencies that can help you plan the perfect vacation. All you need to do is give them an idea of what you want, and let them make it happen for you.

Another awesome aspect of booking a vacation through a travel agency is that, more often than not, these travel agencies offer discounted rates because they are booking so many vacations at once and have standing connections at various hotels and resorts. By using agencies, you can get more out of your vacation than you ever thought possible, and you can likely do so for less money than you would have normally spent. You come out ahead in terms of both time and money.

Actual family time is the other item that takes up a considerable amount of time. However, this is one place in which Done is Better than Perfect absolutely ***does not apply!!!!*** The goal of family time is not to simply get it done and over with. Although I don't yet have any children myself, my friends that do have pointed out that it is often better to spend a shorter amount of very high quality time with their kids than trying to spend larger chunks of lower quality time with them. Consider approaching family time in the same way you would for learning. Dedicate a period of time during which you can comfortably turn off all distractions, including your phone, your email alerts, your TV, or anything else that is not directly relevant to the time you are spending with your family. Just make sure that the time you are spending with your family is truly focused on your family and that you are not splitting your attention.

At the end of the day, you are likely starting a business, at least in part, for them. Don't let them feel left out because you are focusing all of your time on your business. If you are building a puzzle with your daughter, and you spend the entire time not making eye contact, checking texts and emails, replying to her comments with non-committal grunts or "uh huh," it's not going to translate well. She isn't likely to understand at the end of your "time together" why you were so distracted. The time will not be rewarding for you or for her.

If you have been applying this concept to other areas of your life and your business, if you have outsourced activities like shopping, cleaning, cooking, and other time killers, what you will suddenly find is that you have more free time to spend with your family. Therefore, it won't matter if you don't apply DBP to your family, because it won't be necessary. You will have freed up time for them, by applying DBP to other areas of your life.

Take note: your family and your friends are important. Don't leave them behind. Don't let them feel like they are not a priority in your life, because they are a priority. Make sure that they know it.

There are certainly plenty of other areas in your life to which you can apply Done is Better than Perfect. I have given you a starting point for thinking about ways to apply DBP in your own life. Try to think of a few more areas in need of DBP. You will soon realize that almost everything and anything can be outsourced to somebody else in order to free up your time. The best part is that these alternatives often save you money as well. For example, I used to spend almost $100 taking a cab to the airport, but now I spend closer to $45 by hiring an Uber driver for that same trip. That's amazing! I cut my spending by 55% just by finding another method for doing the same activity.

Don't be afraid to apply Done is Better than Perfect to other areas I have not mentioned in this chapter. You will find that the more areas to which you apply this concept, the more time you will be freeing up for other more important parts of your business, your family, and your life.

Check out the link below for a list of fantastic resources to help you outsource parts of your life:

www.outofyourwaybook.com/oustource

CHAPTER EIGHT

Failure And Fear

Failure and fear are the two f-words that matter most.

The word "failure" strikes fear in many minds and hearts. The very idea of it has caused untold millions of would-be entrepreneurs to never even begin their journeys. The dreaded statement, "I'm not angry, I'm just disappointed" comes to mind, as it is usually preceded by a failure. Negative emotions surround and make up the idea of failure; however, I propose that failure, though it should not necessarily be an aspiration, is not a bad thing, especially when it comes to building a business.

The world is littered with people who could be classified as failures but who, through persistence and vision, overcame that stigma and succeeded wildly. Here are a few great examples of "failures" you may not already know:

- **Howard Schultz** – The founder of Starbucks was turned down by 217 of the 242 investors he initially approached. No matter how you may feel about Starbucks, you have to admit it is a wild success.

- **Richard Branson** – The founder of the Virgin brand has started over 100 different companies from phones to records to airlines to condoms; however, only a small handful of his 100 companies has gone on to be successful.

- **Walt Disney** – The iconic Disney brand is known and readily recognized worldwide, and it has inspired millions of raving fans. Despite its clear success, did you know that while working at a newspaper prior to the launch of Disney, Walt Disney was constantly rejected and even told he "lacked imagination"? His first company, a cartoon studio, even went bankrupt after a bad business deal.

These are just a few examples of people who have fit the textbook definition of failure at some point in their lives but have gone on to achieve even greater things because of that failure.

The challenge is to not look at failure as a final destination but as a pit stop on the road to success. There may be many pit stops along that road. There may even be times when it seems as though the road has ended, but perseverance will carry you through. Here are a few beliefs and ways to cope with failures, both in life and in business, and which I offer to you based upon my own experiences:

1. *Haters Gonna Hate*

There are going to be people who will label you as a failure, they are going to call you a failure, they are going to tell you how stupid your idea is, or worse, how stupid you are. These people couldn't be further from the truth. People have a vested interest in keeping you where you are, especially "friends" and family, so when these haters come out of the woodwork to say, "I told you so," ignore them. Don't react to them, and don't give them the satisfaction of getting you worked up over what they are saying. Take the high road, the one that leads to success, and choose not to play in the mud with them. When you turn things around and success arrives, they will be the first ones looking for a piece of the action. I saw a motivational quote once that is fitting for these haters: "If you're not there during my struggles, don't expect to be there for my successes."

2. *Reflect*

Failure is the best opportunity you will have for true learning and growth. Sit down and determine what it is that caused that failure and what you can take away from it. Look at it logically, and try to keep your emotions in check. Write down your conclusions and then review them to help embed what you have learned even deeper into your mindset. Lastly, remember that you have only truly failed if you have learned nothing.

3. Tap into a Mentor

Mentors will be able to provide some of the most valuable advice for when you have failed. Chances are that your mentors will have faced something similar, or if they have not, that they will still have faced some level of failure and overcome that failure. Therefore, they make fantastic sounding boards when you need to bounce ideas off of someone. They can also provide direction after helping you talk through your reflections and draw your conclusions. Most mentors are going to be busy, so make sure that when you contact them to talk, you are not just looking for a shoulder to cry on. Complete the previous steps first, then plug into your mentor channels to help gain a better perspective and receive more fine-tuned advice.

4. Pick Yourself Up

The process of overcoming failure, whether that failure was a personal relationship or a business, a project or a deadline, is one of the most important things you can do. Depending on the size of the failure, your ability to overcome it will vary. It may happen over just a short period of time, or you may find yourself needing a much longer period of time to pick yourself back up. No matter how long the entire process of overcoming failure may take, you must begin that process as soon as possible. Someday, you will look back and think, "That wasn't so bad."

Remember that failure is not a destination; it is just a pit stop along your path to success. Don't let a pit stop hold you back from what you really want in life. Don't let it control what you think you can and cannot do. Own the failure, and make it a part of who you are. Wear it like a badge of honor, because it is, and we all love having a lot of badges!

Eradicate Fear from Your Mind

Now that you know how to overcome failure and be proud of it, you need to address the reason failure has had so much power in your life: fear. Fear is what gives failure power. If you weren't afraid, then failure would simply be an undesirable outcome.

To tackle your fears, you must first address them. Begin by asking yourself the following questions:

- *Did starting your business terrify you even a little bit?*
- *Does it scare you to execute your plans of action?*
- *Does it scare you to ask someone to hand over their money?*
- *Does the idea of success scare you?*

Most people will answer that final question with an emphatic "NO," but when you look at the actions of many entrepreneurs, they demonstrate the exact opposite. You can't possibly start to achieve your definition of success if you are scared of it at a subconscious level and if your brain is helping you avoid taking action.

Fear is an emotional response to something harmful. You are afraid of things that could hurt you, and therefore, fear can be a very necessary emotion. Yes, you should be afraid of that woolly mammoth charging towards you. Yes, you should be afraid of the man with the gun. Yes, you should be afraid of things that will hurt you. Fear is a very necessary emotion in very many situations; however, the state of our existence has risen, and the need for fear in our lives has been dramatically reduced over generations and centuries. If you sit down and really think about it, what exactly in your business could truly hurt you? You may be embarrassed, you may lose money, you may not have the next game-changing idea, or you may even piss some people off. However, none of these things can truly hurt you, and therefore, you shouldn't truly be afraid of anything in your business.

In most businesses, especially in those that are just getting started, the tasks that are necessary to accomplish in order to bring success are often the hardest to tackle. Unfortunately, even if you do accomplish those tasks, success is not a given conclusion. It is possible to execute what you need to do and still not end up at your desired final destination. People will often do more to avoid pain than they will do to gain pleasure. If we agree that success is not guaranteed, then failure is always an option. If you are not careful, your subconscious will use that potential for failure as a rationale for fear. When it does this, it is really saying that because you can't be sure of success, you should do more to avoid that possibility of failure than you should do to seek out success. Your subconscious will cause you to make decisions that will lead you away from that fear, and therefore, your subconscious will cause you to make decisions that will also be leading you away from the potential for success. You may have already reprogrammed your brain to focus on growth with an entrepreneurial mindset, and doing so will help you follow down the right path, but if your brain still fears failure in any way, your subconscious will continue to rise to the surface from time to time and pull you away from your final and successful destinations.

Dune, a novel by Frank Herbert, is focused upon a set of highly trained and specialized people. Whenever they are facing something that they fear, they say the following:

"I must not fear. Fear is the mind-killer. Fear is the little-death that brings total obliteration. I will face my fear. I will permit it to pass over me and through me. And when it has gone past I will turn the inner eye to see its path. Where the fear has gone there will be nothing. Only I will remain."

It is nearly impossible to eliminate fear altogether; however, you can do a lot to control how you perceive fear and overcome it. One of the ways to begin to overcome fear is to incorporate affirmations into your life. Affirmations can be extremely powerful in changing your subconscious and how it thinks.

I have been using affirmations in my daily routine for a few years now, and I have found that they are extremely powerful. Prior to living through the changes they have created, I was the first person to scoff at the idea that simply repeating a few words out loud every day could have an effect at all. If you find yourself feeling the same way, then I propose this simple challenge: incorporate an affirmation into your daily routine for just 30 days. If you don't feel and see a difference after that time period, then you can stop. I think you will be pleasantly surprised.

Now, there are a few basic rules for implementing affirmations successfully. Let's walk through them, so you can set yourself up for a positive affirmation experience.

1. **Say It Out Loud!**

    Repeat the affirmation OUT LOUD every day, both in the morning and at night. Of course, you can do it more than just twice a day if you feel that is necessary.

    Saying an affirmation in your head is great, but when you add in audio stimulation along with your thoughts, your brain takes much more notice. You are receiving the same message through two different points. Repeating that message out loud twice a day increases the effectiveness of what you're saying. I like to have a copy of what I am saying posted in the bathroom as a gentle reminder. At first, you may feel silly repeating your affirmation out loud, but the results will speak for themselves.

2. **Keep it POSITIVE.**

    Negative affirmations can have just as big an impact on your subconscious as positive affirmations can, so don't include anything negative in your affirmation. Keep the statements short, to the point, and positive!

3. **Update your affirmation as necessary.**

    Don't be afraid to change your daily affirmation, though you probably won't want to change it more than once a month. It takes most people about one month from the point of implementing any given affirmation to begin see-ing and feeling differences in their lives. Focus the state-ments you create on areas in which you feel you need to improve your thinking and decision making the most. As those areas change, so too can your affirmations.

With consistent practice and consistent application of this prin-ciple, you will find that things just start coming together. It will al-most seem like stars align in order to get you what you need. When you notice this feeling, what is actually happening is that your sub-conscious has recognized your call for help and is providing you with the mental resources you need for success. Your subconscious will start influencing your decisions based on the information you are feeding it, in a profoundly powerful experience. The following link will provide a list of potential affirmations you may draw from or use as inspiration for creating your own

www.outofyourwaybook.com/afirmations

Another great way to overcome fear and force is to relinquish its control over you by facing the things you fear head on. If you have a fear of heights, go skydiving. If you have a fear of asking for money, work with a charity in which it feels good to ask for money. If you have a fear of public speaking, attend a Toastmasters group to learn excellent communication skills and tips. The idea is simply to find something that will force you to face your fear head on, within an environment that is safe and controlled, in order to help you over-come that fear. Having the support of others while working through this process is absolutely necessary, so buddy up with someone who has the same fears or who has overcome some of their own fears and can act as a guide or mentor.

As you learn how powerless fear really is, and as it loses its hold over you, everything else will get easier. Think of fear as a dry docked boat. You can get on the boat, and it feels comfortable knowing that, because it is not really in the water, there is no danger; you can also never explore, never leave the ground, and never see what else is out there. To defeat fear and truly grow, you MUST exit your comfort zones. You must leave the dry dock behind and set sail for the open sea. Yes, it will be uncomfortable—your "comfort zone" is called that for a reason—and yes, it will mean that you have to do things you may not like to do. Yes, it will mean that you might fail, but it also means that you might succeed, that you might grow, and that you might achieve a higher level of success. Over time, your comfort zone's borders will expand, and a funny thing will happen: you will look back at where you used to be stuck and chuckle at the fears you used to have. You will develop a thrill in expanding your comfort zones, and then, you will truly be free of unnecessary fears.

CHAPTER NINE

Turning Mistakes Into Money

L earning to fail is a unique idea. People often scoff at it and question why they would want to fail, but let's take a moment to consider failure. Begin by reflecting upon the infamous words of Batman's father when he profoundly questions, "Why do we fall? So that we can learn to pick ourselves back up again."

The notion of failure is dependent upon your mindset. If you change your mindset, you can change your perception of what failure is and re-learn what it means to fail. Learn to accept failure as a natural and essential part of growing that allows you to truly set yourself free from the limiting binds of your former beliefs and of perfectionism.

The more you fail, the quicker you can learn and grow from your mistakes. After renovating my first property, I came to learn from my coaches and mentors that I had basically made every mistake I could have made. Each piece of advice was a moment of clarity in which I could do nothing but respond with a sigh, a face-palm, and another mistake tick mark. However, what I learned from those mistakes was invaluable.

Now, I know better, and I can grow faster because I have learned from those mistakes, and I won't make the same mistakes again. My mistakes helped accelerate my learning and growth curve for my real estate business by getting those mistakes out of the way. I will make more mistakes in the future, but now I know that how I respond to those mistakes is a choice I can make. You need to make that choice as well: regret your mistakes and continually beat yourself up over them, or look upon your mistakes with a level of respect, knowing that it is those mistakes, those failures, which are helping you achieve more in your business and helping you grow to be the entrepreneur you are today.

One of the things that set a successful business apart from the rest of the competition is the ability to grow out of failure instead of crumble. You will always make mistakes. Mistakes happen. Whether or not you learn from them is up to you. Of course, learning how to fail is not your end goal, but it is an important part of being a successful entrepreneur and growing a successful business.

Imagine what you can do simply by having a more enlightened view of failure. Imagine how you could grow. Rather than saying, "I can't believe I didn't do that," or "I can't believe I made this mistake," tell yourself, "Well, it sucks that I failed, but I have taken one more step towards finding success and finding a new solution!"

Imagine if, as a kid, you came home, sat down for dinner with your family, and were asked "What did you fail at today?" instead of the obligatory "What did you learn today?" Imagine if you had been judged by your response to failure rather than by your accomplishments. Imagine if your response to failure *was* your accomplishment.

Now, imagine what would happen if you took this approach with your team. What if, when you have your team meetings, you follow up your questions about project victories with questions about project failures? Ask your team what they have failed at, what didn't work, and what they should no longer be doing because they've already attempted it and know it didn't work.

Recently, for the DoneBP.com blog, we decided to expand our audience using paid advertising to attract people just like those reading this book. Prior to this, none of us had very much experience using paid ads in this capacity, so it was a learning experience. The first ad we ran failed miserably. We wasted quite a bit of money and got almost no results. In most cases, people will take that to mean that this strategy doesn't work at all, or their ad was a total failure and they need to start from scratch with something different entirely. Knowing that the first option is unequivocally not true, I determined that I needed to change the ad. However, rather than dramatically changing the entire ad, the target audience, and everything about it, I only changed one small detail. I found, studied, and even copied certain phrases and ideas from ads that I was seeing frequently and knew were working; for example, most of the ads featured an image of a person. My original ad didn't have a person in it, so we added a person. Because I only made one small change, I was able to test how it would impact my bottom line, and I was able to determine with certainty which elements of my ad were working and which were not. If I had completely changed the entire ad, whether or not it worked or didn't work, I would have no idea was causing those changes. By learning and testing to see what works and what doesn't each time, we have developed an ad that outperforms any others. In fact, we are on iteration 25 or so of this particular ad. There were 24 others before this that didn't work as well as number 25, and there will likely be another 25 iterations for us to try! Constant testing and failing are not only important for reaching success, but they are also fantastic for growing your business.

If someone told you, "You messed up. Now, you can figure out how to do it correctly. Nice job!" would it change your perspective on business? Would it change your perspective on life? To err is human; it is in our nature to make mistakes. Imagine if you knew that even in failure your team would have your back and push you to be better. How much more would you accomplish? It is a powerful thing to consider.

If you approach mistakes as growth opportunities, instead of as a process to be feared and avoided at all costs, you could achieve greatness. You could change the entire way our race and planet works simply by asking a different line of questions. Rather than knocking someone down for making a mistake, applaud them for taking a chance, for learning what doesn't work, and for taking one more step towards success.

What would happen if you applied this to everything that you did, not just in your business, but in your life? I challenge you to ask your team, your family, your parents, and your friends, "Where have you made mistakes in your life?" and "What did you learn from those mistakes?" By changing the questions, you can simply yet powerfully change the conversation, and you can change the way people think.

Turn failure into success

I want to share with you a quote I think sums up many entrepreneurs mindsets regarding failure and their innate fear of that failure. Even though this quote was directed at the young folks of the time in which it was written, I think it is still very accurate for today's entrepreneurs. Now, I warn you, it does get a bit wordy, but follow along with me here. It will make more sense in a little bit.

"From my viewpoint, by the greatest challenge facing young people today is that of responding and conforming only to their own most delicately, insistent, intuitive awareness of what the truth seems to them to be as based on their own experiences and not what others have interpreted to be the truth regarding events, which neither they nor others have experienced-based knowledge."

Buckminster Fuller, *Intuition*

Now, I will admit that is a mouthful of a quote! However, I feel it is important and relevant for many entrepreneurs who are stuck in the perpetual cycle of perfection because, too often, opinions of how things should be run in a specific business are founded in conforming to the ideas of people who have no experience in that specific business.

How many people regard a failure in your business as something to be ashamed of or something to hide from? How many people do you know who respond to your failures with "I told you so," "I knew you would," or "Everyone fails in business, and that's why you should never have left your 9 to 5 job"?

I am willing to bet that everyone knows at least a few of these described naysayers; however, you aren't trying to be "everyone." You are trying to be a successful entrepreneur. You are trying to break free from the typical work mold. Ask any successful entrepreneur about your failure, and they will respond, wisely, with a lesson on growth and the value of learning from your mistakes.

Successful entrepreneurs have what Fuller would call experience-based knowledge. These are the folks to which you should be conforming, not the people who lack experience-based knowledge. To put it into more perspective, how many of you, when you first started your business, were met with "bad idea" remarks from your family and friends? How many said things like, "That is a bad market to be in," or "You can't possibly make that restaurant work," or "Don't go into real estate; the market is horrible," or "You have a good job, so why would you risk it to start your own business?"

Those folks don't understand your business. Those folks don't know what you know. Those folks do not have direct experience, and they are basing their information on that lack of experience. They are offering advice and warning based only on things they have heard or that they perceive. Most, if not all, of those folks haven't started their own businesses; they seek comfort and security, rather than taking on risks, despite the rewards that come with them.

You cannot trust their lack of experienced-based knowledge when you are listening to their advice. In fact, you must completely eliminate all of their advice from your life because, more often than not, that "advice," especially if it's not based on experience, will be more detrimental than it will be helpful.

Now, I know that when I say this, many of you will immediately think, "Wait a second. Are you telling me that I can't talk to any of my family or friends ever again?" My answer is, "No. Of course you can talk to your family and friends." I simply mean that if they decide to start providing you with "advice," you have to choose one of two options:

You can simply listen, nod and smile, and completely ignore them. This will make them feel good, as they have a vested interest in keeping you where you are. You know that you are simply listening to be polite, and you can keep in mind that their advice comes from a good place in their heart, even if it comes from a bad place in their mind. The problem with this method is that they will continue to offer you their advice because they think you are listening.

You can tell them, "Hey, I appreciate your opinion. I will definitely take that into consideration; however, I am on a path to success, and I am moving forward with that path on full steam. Perhaps it will mean failure, but as an entrepreneur, I look at failure as one more step towards success. I am secure and confident in the knowledge that I am going to be successful *because* of my failures not in spite of them."

The ironic part about naysayers and their advice is that the moment you do achieve success their tune changes. If you can continue to meet their verbal assault and cynicism with absolute confidence that you cannot fail, because failure is just another point along the path to success, your end victory will be even sweeter.

People like confidence. People follow confidence. Show confidence in what you have. Listen to the people who have already done the things that you have done and who have experience-based knowledge. Know that by doing so, you will have significantly more success, and that any failures you may have already experienced, or that you might experience in the future, can be turned into learning opportunities to help you grow and reach your desired success.

Confidence and devotion to your growth is only one part of this battle however. The other part is having a step by step plan to tackle failure and turn it into success. To help, I have developed a five step system on how to fail towards success. It may seem counterintuitive, and perhaps it is, but I recommend that you implement this system as quickly as possible within your business.

1. Acknowledge the mistake

If you make a mistake, or if a team member makes a mistake, acknowledge that mistake. Own up to the mistake you or your team makes, knowing that, ultimately, as an entrepreneur, any mistake your team makes is your responsibility. You are the one who put your team in charge.

Remember, too, that making the mistake is not the problem. Making the mistake should not make someone feel like they are a failure. It should be a learning process for both you and the team, so don't play the blame game. All the blame game will accomplish is making other people feel worse about working with you and worse about the mistake that was made.

Simply acknowledge the mistake. Stand up and say, "Yes, it's true we made a mistake. We failed. We did something wrong, but that's okay because we've learned new and helpful things along the way." Acknowledging the mistake will allow you and your team to take the next step forward and discover the root cause of that mistake.

2.   Determine the Root Cause

After acknowledging that a mistake has been made, you need to take a step back and look for the root cause of that mistake. There may be a series of actions leading up to the mistake or the failure; however, in most cases, the root cause will not be an action itself, and it will not have immediately preceded the mistake. You may need to look back through your entire process, step by step, from the very beginning to the very end, to find out where it all started to go wrong.

If you fix only mistakes but never causes, mistakes will continue to occur. The mistake itself is a result of other errors; it is never an isolated event. Once you have determined the root cause of the mistake, you can work on correcting that root cause. Use the knowledge you have learned from the mistakes you have made and from the failures you have experienced to help correct the actual problem. Looking for the root cause will allow you to identify the true problem and eliminate the resulting mistakes for good.

3. **Develop and Apply a Fix**

It could be a simple fix. It could be a complicated fix. It could take a very short time to implement. It could take a long time implement. Every mistake and every failure will be different, so again, make sure that you understand the root cause and where you need to apply the fix you have developed.

Keep in mind any corrections you make along your mistake's path, which consists of all of the steps leading from the root cause to the discovered mistake. You will find that it is helpful to map out the process and note where fixes need to be applied. Having this visual representation of the process can help stimulate and generate ideas for fixes as well as help in the process of identifying areas in need of fixing.

4. **Develop and Apply Necessary Course Corrections**

Once the fix has been applied, you will need to develop and apply corrections as necessary to the course of the project in order to get it back on track. Sometimes applying a fix will skew other things in your process, so you need to account for that. Make corrections to the path. Perhaps the mistake will have set you off course for achieving the timeline of your goal, so you will need to be more aggressive in order to make up for that lost time. Whatever the results of your mistake might be, you are going to need to monitor your course, make corrections as necessary, and apply those corrections as necessary.

5. Conduct a 'Post-mistake' Meeting

This is probably the most important step in the process, and yet it is the step most people never do. Instead, they simply apply their corrections and say, "Great! We are on the right path. Let's keep going!" However, it is this evaluation process that is truly the secret to turning failure into success.

Having a post-mistake meeting allows you to understand the mistake, to discuss what was learned through that process, and to brainstorm how you can avoid similar mistakes in other processes down the road. Only through growth and reflection can you truly work to eliminate mistakes and failures.

A post-mistake meeting should be conducted for every mistake warranting one. Now, if the mistake was simple, like someone transposing a number incorrectly or something of that nature, you don't necessarily have to run through all of these five steps. However, you do need to apply this five step system to larger mistakes and to failures in projects and businesses that have impacted the bottom line.

You will need to define where and when this process makes sense in your business. You have the tools to tackle your mistakes, so now you need to apply them. With this simple five step system, you can start to achieve significantly higher results and start to fail towards success, which is a great path for your business.

Bonus Growth Opportunity

For those who really want to grow at an accelerated pace, I have one more out-of-the-box idea for you to implement: a periodic failure report. Usually, when I talk about this, people's eyes grow wide and they say, "Wait, you want me to report on failure? That makes no sense. You're crazy if you think I am going to report every time I have failed!" People who think this way often have a fixed mindset.

They are stuck in the idea that if they are failing, they are doing something bad. They haven't implemented a failure to success methodology in their company.

Your business' leadership should document the growth of any employees or of any contractors on your team, in your business, or working with your business, based on the mistakes that they have made, and it should be done as soon as possible. Periodically, everyone on your team should be required to submit a list of all their failures, and it should also include what they learned from each of those failures and how they can benefit the company.

Now, this is important: **under no circumstance should this list be used to berate, belittle, demean, or otherwise bring down an employee.** It should provide a means by which to measure your team's growth because your team's growth is ultimately your business' growth. Team members who are required to document their mistakes and resulting knowledge will see dramatic growth by leaps and bounds. Realizing that failure is okay, as long as something is learned from it, will free their minds, and it will give them the confidence to put their best foot forward. They will no longer feel scared to try new ideas. They will feel secure, knowing that if they do fail it will be treated as a growth opportunity and not as a detriment to the project or business.

Periodic reports will also provide reference documentation for new employees who may have similar ideas, thereby lessening their learning curve and increasing the overall success of everyone on your team. Accompanied by your list of failures, you can say, "That's a great idea, and I appreciate it, but we tried it here, and this was the result. If you think there is a different way of going about it to achieve a better result, we are open to that. Otherwise, we have learned that it doesn't work, and here's why, so we are going to stick with what we have right now."

If the idea has not been tried, then let them try it. After all, what's the worst that can happen? If the idea fails, you can return to the way you were doing it before, and you will have learned a bit more in the process. You will be able to say, "I have found one more way that doesn't work, so we are all one step closer to discovering a way that can succeed." If the idea works, not only will that team member feel an immense satisfaction from developing a winning idea, but you will all see the results of that idea.

After implementing periodic failure reports in your business, please share the results of those reports. I would love to hear how they are used in your business, so share your experiences on our Facebook page (facebook.com/donebp) or on our webpage (outofyourwaybook.com). Let us know if you have implemented periodic failure reports and how they have worked for your business.

CHAPTER TEN

Overcoming Perfection

L et's talk about how to overcome perfection and start getting rid of a mindset that has been built into your brain over the last 20 or more years. I want to warn you: It won't be easy. It was not easy for me, and for those of you who have to overcome 20 years of programming, it will be an even tougher task to accomplish.

You will struggle with it. You are not simply going to just "change your mind" and watch everything improve. Changing your mindset will take time. It takes time to get results, and it takes time for you to see those results in your business, but over time it will become second nature. You will have reprogrammed yourself for more success.

Keep that in mind as you move forward. Don't get frustrated or discouraged if you don't have immediate results. As is the case for most things in life, the best experiences often require the biggest struggles and offer the greatest challenges. As you develop new thought patterns, you will start to notice that it does work and works very well. The transformation will begin with small things at first, such as your mood and how you feel each day, and it will transform over time into bigger things like your business' success.

One of the easiest ways to overcome perfection is by outsourcing. Now, when I start talking about outsourcing, I immediately expect some eye rolls and some grumbling, but I don't necessarily mean sending jobs to foreign countries. What I mean is that you should begin removing items off of your business plate by giving them to someone else.

That someone else could be in your office, in a different city, or even in a different country. I don't really care where the person is. I care more about the results they will achieve and what those results will cost because I'm running a business. If I'm going to be successful, I'm going to need to do what makes sense for my business.

Realize that when people give outsourcing a negative connotation, more often than not, they are thinking about companies laying off employees in order to hire cheaper employees in other countries.

For most of you, this does not apply, but do realize that it is okay to pull in people from other countries, or anywhere else, because if your business doesn't make it, no one is going to be working for you in any location.

Do the right things for your business, instead of trying to do the right things for everybody else. If you constantly try to live up to others' expectations, you will constantly find yourself failing.

What can you outsource?

You can outsource anything and everything. If there is something you are doing in your business, you can outsource it. I could even outsource the writing of this book if I wanted to. Now, of course, it wouldn't have my tone, and it wouldn't have my style. It would seem very distant for those who know me well; however, for most readers, all that would matter is the great content.

Let's think about what kinds of things, specifically, can be outsourced. The first thing to look at is anything you hate doing or are not as good at doing. You have expertise in some areas, and you lack expertise in some areas. Understanding where you have this expertise and where you don't is important to your business. If you don't take the time to figure out what it is that you are good at, all you are doing is setting yourself up to fail or be miserable because your business will become a job rather than a passion.

Take a look at the things you don't like doing. Take a look at the things you don't like spending time on and outsource those things first. They will be the easiest to outsource because you don't really want to do them anyway. They will also be the things that are least likely to get done on your task list because you'll keep putting them off in favor of things you do enjoy doing.

Once you've handed over the unpleasant aspects of your business, consider outsourcing the following:

1. **Writing**

Outsource writing, especially if you are not a profes-
sional writer. Much of what you do in business is about creating content. Content is what allows people to see what
you have to offer, why you are offering it, how you are offering it, and what you are bringing to the table. Content
includes things like blog posts, white papers, marketing fly-
ers, etc. Any form of writing can usually be outsourced, and
it can usually be outsourced for a much lower rate than you
would be charging for your own time.

2. **Graphic design**

Another thing to consider outsourcing is graphic design.
Now, if you are a designer, and you like designing things, I
completely understand if you don't want to outsource this
task. However, you need to realize that even if you are a
good graphic designer, and you know how to do it, that
doesn't mean that you should. As business owners, you
should be outsourcing any activity with a low dollar per
hour rate, and many graphic designers can be obtained for
less than $20 an hour. Your time is worth significantly
more than $20 an hour. Don't waste it.

3. **Accounting/Bookkeeping**

The next tasks to consider outsourcing are accounting
and bookkeeping. Now, there are some vital factors to consider while deciding whether or not to outsource accounting. For example, how trustworthy is the person you are
hiring? The last thing you want to find out is that he or she
has been embezzling money from your company, or forget-

ting to pay important business taxes, but you weren't very good at accounting, so you didn't even notice.

Accounting is usually one of those areas in which you will be well advised to seek outside opinions. Talk to other entrepreneurs, friends, contacts, and people who you know within your network, to find out who they are using and what their reputation is.

Accounting can be outsourced, but take some time to consider what it is that you are outsourcing and how important it is to your business, before handing over your records.

4. **Technical tasks**

Again, some of you reading this are thinking, "I can write code," "I can build webpages," "I can design Word-Press themes," or whatever other technical task you may be capable of doing. That is all fine and dandy, but again, you can obtain most technical folks for less than $20 an hour, and that means you are valuing yourself at $20 an hour or less. As business owners, you should be valuing your time at a much higher rate.

5. **Repetitive Tasks**

Any time you find yourself doing the same thing over and over and over again, consider outsourcing it. Whoever takes over this task for you will be happy to do so. He or she will have a steady source of income by taking on these tasks, and more often than not, you will be able to pay a significantly lower dollar per hour rate than what your own time is worth.

6. Low Wage Tasks

Consider outsourcing anything that you can hire someone to do for a low wage. This could include cleaning crews, grounds maintenance (i.e. lawn care and snow shoveling), security, and other tasks like this. There are lots of local businesses that you can support that will tackle these low wage tasks for your business and leave you free to focus on revenue generating activities.

These are just a few of the many tasks you can outsource. Take a look at every task you are doing in your business. If you really enjoy doing it, then keep doing it, but keep in mind that your business does need to generate revenue, and sometimes you may even need to hand over the enjoyable tasks in order to grow the business. It's your business, and you can do what you want to do within your business, but if you don't like doing it, you should definitely consider outsourcing it.

There are thousands of websites to help you find people to do any kind of task you can possibly imagine. I have taken the time to keep an up-to-date list of places you can find virtual assistants. Please head to the following link in order to learn the latest and greatest

www.ourofyourwaybook.com/outsource

Once you have identified a place to find and hire help within your business, you need to identify which people and companies are good and which people are bad. The next link will take you to a page on how to go about hiring people. It is not the focus of this book, but I think it is important to know how to locate and identify good team members outofyourwaybook.com/team

Remember that your time is valuable. If a task isn't worth your time, why are you still doing it?

CHAPTER ELEVEN

Achieving Hyper-Focus

One of the biggest problems with entrepreneurs is staying focused, not on a goal, but on an activity, maintaining hyper-focus for a short period of time. By learning how to hyper-focus your attention, you can blaze through projects and get more done in less time. This is especially valuable when the focus is on a revenue generating activity!

Here are some guidelines to keep you better focused on your tasks at hand:

1. **Understand how you work**

   Everyone has his or her own tricks for getting work done. Personally, I like to have music on while I'm working, and I have found that heavy bass music with a great upbeat tempo, but not very many words, which I find distracting, is my preferred choice. I also enjoy Ke$ha. Now, I know many of you might be thinking: "Whaaat?!" Let me explain. I love her music, and if you have ever seen her perform, you know that she gives everything she has to her music. I find that level of dedication to be inspirational. If you feel inspired while you are focusing, you are going to see better results.

   On the opposite end of the sound spectrum, there are people who need complete silence in order to stay focused. Perhaps, you are one of these people. If there is any music playing, you will not be able to accomplish any work at all. Know who you are.

   In addition to music, proper lighting can be important as well. I like to have mellow yet sufficient lighting in the room. Florescent lights kill my vibe quickly, yet others find them soothing.

No matter what your work environment choices may be, understand what it is that keeps you on track, and use it. Don't be afraid to set your own mood, ambiance, or vibe within your workplace in order to help you accomplish more and do so efficiently. The more aligned the environment is to your personal needs, the more hyper-focused you will be able to become. If you are unsure of what your needs are, experiment until you find your ideal fit.

2. Turn off distractions

This is critical!! You must—not "should"—you MUST turn off the following:

a. Email

Email is probably the single largest distraction for anyone in any business, and it is a horrible time killer. When you want to stay hyper-focused, shut down your email. Turn off your notifications, close the window on your computer, and let those emails wait until the end of your hyper-focused session.

b. Telephone

Put ALL of your phone notifications on silent, or if you are unable to do so, be sure to shut off or put your phone out of sight in order to not be distracted by lights that flash or a screen that turns on periodically. Your hyper-focused time is your time; it is not to be spent on anyone else. These periods are not going to last very long or for any extended period of time, so anyone who calls you can leave a voicemail. You can respond to any messages as soon as you have finished your hyper-focused session.

Most hyper-focused sessions are going to last for 15 to 30 minutes, with that upper limit being much less frequent. Whoever leaves you a voicemail during that time period will still be responded to shortly, so even in the event of an emergency, you will be able to return contact within a very reasonable amount of time. Don't worry about what is happening in the outside world. Worry instead about what you are working on within any given hyper-focused session.

c. Social media

When I say "social media," I do mean all forms of social media. Facebook, Pinterest, Instagram, SnapChat, Twitter, or any other outlet you may use, must be off limits during your hyper-focused session. Social media can be a huge distraction if you let it become one, but if it is out of sight, it is often out of mind. Remember, all of these social networks, and all of the notifications that go along with them, will still be there when you are ready to check them. Just don't give in to that temptation during your hyper-focused session.

d. Friends, family, roommates, etc.

If you are working in a location in which you are easily reachable, then you need to lay down a few ground rules. Let these people know that it is not okay to disturb you if the door is closed. It is not okay to bother you, even if they are only intending to ask you a "quick question." It is not okay to stop in, even if they are offering to take down a lunch request. During a hyper-focused session, it is not okay to disturb you for any reason, unless, of course, the building is burning down. Although these interruptions may only seem minor to them, they are, in fact, massive distractions that will cause you to lose focus, thereby decreasing the positive results of being hyper-focused.

3. Break your hyper-focused sessions into reasonable chunks.

Everyone can stay focused for different periods of time. I challenge you to figure out how much time you can focus and still remain effective. For most of you, that period of time is only going to be for 15 to 30 minutes, but however long works for you, stick to that. After each session, make sure you take a break for at least ten minutes. Get a drink of water. Do five quick push-ups. Use the restroom. Take a brisk walk down the hall. Stand and stretch in front of a window while admiring the view. Let your brain reset, and let yourself get ready for another hyper-focused session.

During this "downtime," you can also do things like respond to emails, return phone calls, and answer any "quick questions." Your hyper-focused time is not the time for these activities.

4. Set a task for each hyper-focused session

Select one thing you want to focus on getting done or accomplishing per session, and go to town on it. It is the only thing you will work on during that single hyper-focused session. There will be no other activities, tasks, or things to complete during that session. By selecting just one specific task, you will be better able to focus on it and to complete it. If that one thing is going to require more time than you have the ability to stay hyper-focused, break that thing into smaller chunks, and address them one at a time until you have completed the larger goal.

5. Reward yourself

After you have successfully accomplished the goal your hyper-focused session was meant to achieve, reward yourself. Perhaps your reward will be something small, like going to get that latte. Perhaps your reward will be something big, like going out to dinner with friends.

The specific reward is not as important as being able to hold yourself accountable for your goal and focusing your time on achieving and sticking to that goal. At the end of the day, you will feel much more success in having reached your goal than you will from any reward.

After implementing these hyper-focus sessions throughout your day, you are going to find the results to be quite staggering. The world has given us so many distractions that you may even come to enjoy your time away from everything. Engage in as many of these sessions as you can each day for maximum results and maximum productivity. Before you know it, you will be the Yoda (a master) of hyper focus!

CHAPTER TWELVE

Get Out Of Your Own Way!

This is the shortest chapter in the book, but it is also the most important one. No one will know the exact statistic, but I wager that a staggering number of people who read this book cover to cover will not do a single thing I have advised. An even larger number of readers will never make it to this chapter. Even more people will never pick up this book at all, fearing that they will have to change.

You have made it to this final chapter! You have read all of the previous chapters! I sincerely congratulate you. You have made it into a small group of dedicated entrepreneurs who are willing to make positive changes, and you should be proud of this accomplishment.

Of course, no amount of congratulations and yay-rah-rah in the world will help you if you don't actually act. If you don't try out a single of your newly learned ideas, tasks, and philosophies, then what was the point of dedicating your time to reading about them? I challenge you to implement just one item shared with you and to see what happens. I am willing to bet you will quickly implement even more!

I also challenge you to share your results. Share them with us, and share them with your friends, your family, your fellow entrepreneurs, or with anyone at all! Some of the most influential mentors I have had in my life taught me to "Celebrate All Wins" (CAW). They have also dedicated an entire website to help their students celebrate their wins with the world. A win could be something as small as finally approving the final version of my logo, or it could be something as big as a six figure deal. The idea is to feel good every time something positive takes place. This rewarding behavior reinforces positive things in your life and helps you feel great about where you are heading. Plus, you get to run around yelling at the top of your lungs, "CAW! CAW! CAW!"

That's it folks! You have all the tools necessary to Get Out Of Your Own Way now! I encourage you to utilize the resources outlined in this book and check out the bonus materials and tools located on the website!

ABOUT THE AUTHOR

Bob McIntosh grew up in an entrepreneurial family that forged his passion for building and scaling businesses. His dad taught him through his own actions that hard work and determination are the best combination to achieve your dreams. His mom taught him how to be compassionate and listen to people which is a critical skill for entrepreneurs often overlooked. Since graduating college he has built several successful businesses and helped thousands scale and build their own dream businesses. The first business he started was a real estate investing business he began with his dad in the Buffalo NY market. They're still very active in the residential redevelopment market and love providing solutions for all sorts of real estate needs in that market. From there Bob's passion for technology came to the forefront. Recognizing the power of the internet Bob then dove into internet marketing, affiliate marketing, and information product development. He was instrumental in building and launching numerous products that have generated tens of thousands of dollars of passive income over the last several years. From there Bob found his true passion in helping other entrepreneurs learn and grow from the mistakes and struggles that he and so many others face. He has spoken on stages in front of thousands of entrepreneurs all across the country, has personally coached one on one and through high level mastermind events numerous entrepreneurs to greater levels of success and revenue in their own businesses. Connect with him at http://outofyourwaybook.com

Made in the USA
Charleston, SC
10 December 2015